GOD PROVIDES

Life Lessons from God

One Man's Experience

George L. Yates

Foreward by: Dr. Frank Cox

i

Published by Sonlight Publishing

SonC.A.R.E. Ministries

Christ's Awareness Raised Everyday

Website: soncare.net

ISBN: 978-0-9988852-6-1

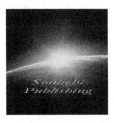

What others are saying about God Provides

George Yates has a gift for observing routine daily experiences and learning a significant life lesson, but more importantly, he's willing to share those life lessons with us. His ability to tell stories in a succinct and rich manner always draws me in when I see a blog post or article with his byline. Now we have a book full of his edifying and easy-to-follow, real-life experiences — one person's life lessons that can help all of us grow in a variety of ways. Thank you for sharing these stories with us, George. And thank you for challenging us to reflect on our own life experiences. *Jennifer Davis Rash, President and Editor-in-Chief, TAB Media and The Alabama Baptist*

God Provides: Life Lessons from God, By George Yates, is both challenging and inspiring. This book is filled with hope and possibilities. You journey with George through real life struggles, hurts, and victories. Through it all, he points you to a God who loves you and is working all things for good. Read it to be encouraged. Read it to be motivated. Perhaps more than anything, read it to be reminded of what God can and will do through your life for His glory. *Rob Jackson, Director, Office of Church Health, Alabama Baptist State Board of Missions*

"Thank you for the opportunity to read your book in advance and I know it will be a blessing to many. I read it with great delight and interest. I believe this book will be inspiration to many." *Dr. Mark D. Berry, Ed.D, District Superintendent, Central Gulf Coast District Church of the Nazarene.*

"Some books educate you. Many books enlighten you. The best of books educate, enlighten, and inspire you. The words found in this book, written by my friend George, will accomplish all three. By telling his story, he unearths the heart of our faithful God. By merely telling when and how God worked in his own life, he'll enhance yours. You'll laugh some, and you may cry some. But most of all, you'll be in awe of God who cares. If you choose to give the time necessary to read this book, I can assure you that you will be educated and enlightened, but most of all, YOU WILL BE INSPIRED!" *Rick Howerton, Regional Consultant, South Central Region, Kentucky Baptist Convention*

"This book is a powerful reminder that God is a faithful God and we can count on Him to guide and provide. These pages have challenged me to more closely listen to God's voice, follow His lead, and trust in His provisions. If you need a faith-lift, this book will give it!" *Daniel Wilson, Director, Office of Evangelism, Alabama Baptist State board of Missions*

"According to George Yates, 'God's calling on our lives is to follow him.' With all the ups and downs life hands us, to stay in step with the Lord is the only way to bear fruit. *God Provides* is an incredible tool to help us on the journey of life." *Dr. Robert Mullins, Lead Pastor of crossroads Community Church, Elmore, Alabama, Executive Director of PassionTree.org Pastors Network*

"Through a series of personal experiences, George leads the reader back into the truths of Scripture. He reminds us of God's faithfulness, provision, and care for his followers. No matter what season of life you find yourself in, I believe you will find this book encouraging and refreshing. It was a great reminder to me that I have a God that meets me where I am and works in ways that are sometimes beyond our comprehension." *Chad Keck, Ph.D., Senior Pastor, FBC Kettering, OH*

"George Yates in, GOD PROVIDES: *Life Lesson's From God, One Man's Journey,* tells how God has been faithful in being Jehovah Jireh, God who provides. George has found God faithful to provide monthly bills, key people for positions in ministry, employment at the right time, help in the midst of chronic pain, and open doors for serving Christ. Any reader who is struggling with whether they can trust the Lord will find great encouragement in hearing the story of George's journey. God is faithful and He is indeed Jehovah Jireh, God who provides." *Dr. Todd Gray, Executive Director-Treasurer, Kentucky Baptist Convention*

Contents

Acknowledgements

Many thanks to Dr. Frank Cox for the beautifully written foreword reminding us of God's working through the life of David in good times and bad. Thank you for challenging us to watch for God as we read each chapter and as we walk each day of life. You are a blessed man, and I am blessed to know you.

To the eight men and women who read the manuscript and contributed words of encouragement and endorsement. (*Reader: Be sure to go back and read their words especially if you skipped over them. God used them in preparing this book.*) You are each a blessing to me, and God sent into my life.

To my life partner, my wife Pam. Without you by my side, loving, supporting, and encouraging me – and sometimes slowing me down, I might have missed some of God's life lessons. You are indeed a prayer warrior, a woman seeking God's heart, and God's best in my life. I love you!

To my wife Pam and Jessica Ingram for the editing, Pam with the first edit and Jessica with the final edit. If not for you errors would have been missed.

To the many men and women God has used over the years to teach, train, and equip me to be his faithful servant. I fall short each day, but God has used many in my life to equip, encourage, and lift my arms (Exodus 17) through daily struggles and battles. I am eternally grateful to God for each one.

To you the reader, thank you for desiring enough to pick this book up and read it. I am grateful to you and pray that God will use the writings found inside to inspire you to be watchful of and to share God's life lessons to you.

Foreword

The person who does not learn from life's lessons is destined for a long, unproductive life. I learned early in life that no one is perfect. Well, there was one and He was Jesus. Outside of Him, we all have endured trials and made mistakes that turned into teachable moments. Some missteps in life carried little consequences while others carried severe effects. We all have been on the altar of such experiences.

One of the greatest men in the Word of God is David. Every day he impacts my life. You read it right, David. He was the one who was out in his father Jessie's field watching over those bleating sheep, communing with God. It had to be a rich time for David because out of those experiences where God provided for him, he produced the powerful wisdom we read in the book of Psalms. Remember, God's Word describes him as a man after the heart of God (Acts 13:22). How could this be? Simple. David did whatever God wanted him to do. Obedience!

He endured trials of his own that prepared him for life's battles. It produced wisdom in David's life. David learned his lessons and how to depend upon God. I am sure we all can recite one trial where God taught us life lessons to be learned and passed on.

Think with me about a particular moment in David's life. He was about to go into battle against the giant Goliath. King Saul, who, by the way, was not at the front of the line to join the battle himself, questioned David's suitability for the fight. Saul looked at him and declared, "You are but a youth, and he is a man of war from his youth!" (1 Sam.17:33). Then David explained he was prepared by God for such a time as this (v. 34).

"When the words that David spoke were heard, they informed Saul, and he sent for him. And David said to Saul, 'May no one's heart fail on account of him; your servant will go and fight this Philistine!' But Saul said to David, 'You are not able to go against this Philistine to fight him; for you are *only* a youth, while he has been a warrior since his youth.' But David said to Saul, 'Your servant was tending his father's sheep. When a lion or a bear came and took a sheep from the flock, I went out after it and attacked it, and rescued *the sheep* from its mouth; and when it rose up against me, I grabbed *it* by its mane and struck it and killed it. Your servant has killed both the lion and the bear; and this uncircumcised Philistine will be like one of them, since he has defied the armies of the living God.' And David said, 'The Lord who saved me from the paw of the lion and the paw of the bear, He will save me from the hand of this Philistine.' So, Saul said to David, 'Go, and may the Lord be with you.' (1 Sam. 17:31-37, NASB, emphasis added).

In this passage, I can hear David saying, "The Lord and my life experiences have prepared me for success in this battle." Isn't that the way it happens? A pivotal moment comes our way (a life experience), and God takes such a moment and teaches powerful lessons that produce wisdom in us. Such wisdom is never to be hidden or held close to the vest but is to be shared so others can succeed and achieve in their daily life. Through his lion and bear experience, David taught me to totally rely upon God. He taught me not to commit adultery because it destroys. He taught me not to cover sin because it carries serious consequences. So much from life experiences did David teach. We can learn from him!

We can and must learn from others. Miguel de Cervantes Saavedra writes, "Time ripens all things; no man is born wise." Over the years I picked up another jewel of wisdom: "Everything we meet in life becomes a part of us!" We learn from every encounter in life.

George Yates does a masterful job in *God Provides* to use real life stories and Scripture that has molded his life. Each of these stimulates one to look for God in every circumstance we meet on our journey. God is present and at work in and around us. He uses others to help us find direction. God has a wonderful plan for each of us and will move heaven and earth as we obey Him. God uses what He must to move us on this continuum called life in which we set out to accomplish His will and to glorify His name.

Here is my hope: With every chapter you read, God will encourage you. Look for God's presence through George's real-life experiences of walking the faith journey. You will begin to see that God is at work and see how He works. Also, be mindful as you are encouraged by others. He is molding you to be an encourager to those in your sphere of influence. You may just end up being God's presence for someone else. May it be!

Dr. Frank Cox, Pastor's Study,
North Metro Baptist Church, Lawrenceville, Georgia

Introduction

Thank you for picking up this book to read. My prayer is that God will use what he has allowed me to write in these pages to encourage you in your journey and your spiritual walk of life. When I read the entries in this book, I am filled with joy at the reflection of the experiences, the many people He has brought into my life, and the lessons He has taught me through each one. Perhaps you are one of those people. If so, thank you!

Maybe it is my personality type or a behavioral trait, but nonetheless I am grateful for the ability to recognize God at work in my life and distinguish lessons from Him in my life experiences. Granted, God has taught me many more lessons than this book can contain, and I have likely missed some of God's experiences. Still, I am ever mindful and observant, watching for God in my circumstances and trying to remain open to learning from each one.

Some of life's lessons are learned through pain, be it physical, mental, or spiritual discomfort. Some are learned through trial and hardship, and others through joy and conquest. God can use any circumstance to stretch and to teach you. This is how we mature as disciples of Christ. Each lesson, even in pain, is a valuable treasure.

Writing these stories from my life brought memories of several other experiences as well. Some happy, some sad. Some experiences and lessons need not be shared. They are valuable and distinct to me alone. Other lessons I have learned will likely go to the grave with me — experiences that still grieve me after many years because I now know the anguish and sorrow that I caused my Lord in my disobedience. I am grateful that I serve a God of forgiveness and mercy.

After reading this book I pray you will sit down and reflect on some of your life's experiences. Write them down along with the lessons learned. Share them with others. Learn to be watchful and teach others to be watchful as well, as the Lord attempts to teach you on your life's journey.

Our God provides not only financially or materialistically. With each trial, situation, and circumstance, God provides a learning experience.

The Hebrew phrase for "God provides" is Jehovah-Jireh. God provides!

Growth Never Takes Place in Your Comfort Zone

At age twenty-one, I had a sporting accident that shredded all the ligaments behind my left knee so badly, I was told, they could not be surgically repaired. In the same accident, I also tore a bleeding cartilage. After a painful week where the knee had to be drained of internal bleeding three times, I had the surgery to remove the bleeding cartilage followed by four to six weeks in a soft cast. The next steps of recovery included eight weeks of rigorous workouts at a physical therapy clinic and at home.

My therapist, Becky, as I recall, was nice enough. She was not very big, but she sure knew how to bend, torque, and maneuver my leg to the point of deep pain. I will not say that she took pleasure in delivering me to my threshold of pain, but I do believe I saw a smile on her face while putting me through those rigors. I took the rehab seriously, and faithfully worked to strengthen that knee and leg.

My range of motion with that leg on my first visit was less than twelve degrees, barely bendable. For those old enough to remember, I walked like Chester on Gunsmoke. The day I left therapy for the final time, the range was nearing 120 degrees. When my eight weeks were finished, the personnel at the rehab center said I had gone farther than any patient they had ever seen, including some twice my size. I had set a goal of the amount of weight I would work out with on my final day, and through perseverance I reached that goal. The goal I set was based on a number my surgeon had stated. Later, I realized he used that number figuratively to say, reach as far as you can. And I did.

My physical therapist taught me how to do a series of exercises to strengthen my left leg that would take forty- to forty-five minutes each day. The first time was without weights. Then we strapped a one-pound weight around my ankle. The next day two, then three ... On my last day, I completed that same workout with forty pounds of weight strapped to my ankle. Little skinny me, maybe 129 pounds, had successfully completed all the required exercises with forty pounds of weight around my ankle. Unbeknownst to me at the time, it was a sight and feat never before accomplished at the physical therapy center.

My therapist and other center personal told me that day that only one patient had ever tried that much weight before. In their words, "And he was a big, strong cop, at least twice your size."

When I walked out of that center for the final time my left leg was much stronger than the right leg, which had never been damaged.

I went through a lot of painful workouts and painful days during that time. I did it because I had a goal in mind. I was going to be as strong as I was before the accident. To my surprise, I came out stronger.

We all face trials, struggles, and hardships in life. There will be physical ones, like what I faced. There also will be financial hardships, mental struggles, and even spiritual trials too. When we go through life's struggles, trials, and hardships, God leads us through them, so we will come out stronger believers and stronger proponents for His Kingdom and His power.

The first chapter of the book of James tells us, "Consider it a great joy, my brothers, whenever you experience various trials, knowing that the testing of your faith produces endurance. But endurance must do its complete work, so that you may be mature and complete, lacking nothing" (James 1:2–4, HCSB).

If I had laid around crying about my poor knee and how it couldn't be surgically repaired, if I had not worked out daily as instructed by my therapist, my knee would have atrophied worse than during the five weeks in the soft cast following surgery. It would have been a useless knee, not able to carry my own weight.

I had to stretch it, work it, bend it, lift weights with it, and let the physical therapist bend it until I was in deep pain. My leg had to be stretched beyond what was comfortable. My rehabilitation of that leg was not a one-time venture. No, it was day by day, every day for at least one thirty- to forty-five-minute workout each day. Some days I put in two forty-five-minute workouts.

So it is in life. If you want to grow, you've got to be stretched — sometimes until it hurts. It is a day-by-day process of development. Growth never takes place in your comfort zone. God stretches us to strengthen us. The more we are stretched, the more intense our workout, the stronger we become.

When a man accepts this testing in the right way, and day by day develops this steadfast devotion moving through each day, then day by day he will live more triumphantly and draw nearer to the standard of Jesus Christ Himself.

Jehovah Jireh, God is my provider.

More Month Than Income?

When my wife, Pam, and I were dating, early in our relationship, we both worked second shift at a hospital. We would often make plans to do something together before going to work — lunch dates or morning excursions. One morning, Pam arrived at my house while I was paying bills. I calculated everything and realized I was going to be short $145 for the month. Even though there were still two weeks left in the month, I realized I was not going to have enough income to pay all my bills.

I proceeded to write checks for those bills with the earliest due date. However, before writing any of those, the first check I wrote was to my church. That check was a tithe, ten percent of everything I had earned (gross earnings) so far that month. Looking over my shoulder, Pam stated, "You can't do that. You don't have enough money."

I turned in my chair to face her and said, "I cannot afford not to," and I proceeded to write the other checks. She attempted to reason with me — from her perspective — but I continued. I was raised in a home and church where we were taught tithing, giving a tenth of every income into your home, was biblical and the right thing to do, so I was compelled to write the tithe check first. After all, I had seen some amazing fruit of this teaching and practice in the lives of others, including my father. I believed it because God had proven Himself to me in tithing. And I realized Pam had not had the pleasure of knowing this truth, yet.

One of those amazing experiences happened just a few years prior to this particular morning. My father was forced into medical retirement at age 49 due to heart issues. At one point, his Social Security was cut off. With no pension, this was all the income Dad had. My mother worked, but they needed Dad's Social Security too. With no idea when he would receive another check, Dad wrote a $50 check to the church — his tithe.

To many people, Dad could've had a "pass" since the government was auditing his account. But not to Dad. He was a tither. He knew God would take care of him. Dad had recently been in the hospital, and leaving church that day a friend handed Dad a greeting card envelope. Dad assumed it was another get well soon or encouragement card. When he got to the car, he opened the envelope and indeed there was a card of encouragement inside, along with a $50 bill. The greatest encouragement was not the card or the $50 bill. It was the wonder of God providing the exact amount Dad had written for his offering check.

Two days after my bill paying experience with Pam, I received in the mail a bill I had not calculated. I had not expected it. This additional debt was for $23.35. I was glad Pam wasn't around that morning to remind me that my shortfall for the month was now going to be $168.35. Though I did tell her about it later.

Less than one week after receiving the additional bill, I received another unexpected envelope in the mail. Inside this second surprise envelope was a check for some photography work I had done more than a year before. Because I had not received payment when it was due, I had, in my mind, written this long overdue payment off months before. The check in the envelope that morning totaled $168.75.

God knew what I needed to pay all my bills that month. He even included the amount for the additional outstanding bill of $23.35 that I had not yet received when I wrote the tithe check. I could not have known the amount, but God did. And He made arrangements to fulfill all of my financial obligations that month. God's timing is always perfect, and His provision is always exactly what you need. In this case, and to show God has a sense of humor, He even gave me an extra forty cents. Enough for the postage stamp needed to mail the extra bill that month.

A very familiar Scripture passage to many churchgoers is Malachi 3:10: "'Bring all the tithes into the storehouse, that there may be food in My house, And try Me now in this,' says the LORD of hosts, 'If I will not open for you the windows of heaven And pour out for you such blessing, that there will not be room enough to receive it'" (NKJV).

I learned, even as a child, to put God first in everything and He will supply for all your needs. The greatest learning experience that day was not that God provided for me (though that was huge). The greatest experience was what Pam learned. In thirty-plus years together since that morning she has never questioned first giving to God and watching Him take care of the rest. She learned one of God's great promises that day. A life-long lesson of stewardship and God's blessings. Only a few days ago, I heard her recanting the lesson from that day to another person. I am glad in heart each time I hear her share that story with someone. One comment in her recent discussion, "There is no way I would not tithe."

The Lord will provide, just as Abraham found out and is recorded in Genesis 14, and as Pam found out when we were dating.

Jehovah Jireh – God is my provider.

Trust God and Place Your Future in His Hands

Troubled and perplexed, I needed to talk with someone. It seemed to me that I was stuck in a dead-end job. I was looking for something else, something better. My fiancé and I would be getting married in less than a year and I needed a better means of support. Also, I wanted to use my skills and God-given abilities. That was not happening in my current job. I loved and was loved by the people I worked with and was satisfied with my work production, but the personal challenge was missing.

I sent my resume out for a few positions. One particular company called for an interview. I agreed, set up times, and went through a series of interviews for a management position in a large retail organization. In the first set of interviews, it was disclosed that to enter the management training program with this company, you had to have a college degree or work your way up within the company from an entry-level position in one of their stores. I had neither, so I marked that one off my mental list.

You can imagine my surprise a few days later when I received a call offering me the position — in Ohio. Though surprised, I did not mention my shortcomings to their qualifications. They offered, I accepted. That is, I accepted, until I got cold feet. I began to question my decision. I knew the company. They had stores right there in my hometown. I shopped with them often. But what if they found out their mistake and withdrew the offer. What if I truly couldn't make it? I mean, after all, I did not have a college degree. Could I leave my family and my fiancé? That was why I needed to talk to someone.

I called a friend, Barbara Wooden. Barbara was, in my opinion, a righteous, godly woman. We taught Bible study to junior high students at Highland Park First Baptist Church in Louisville, Kentucky. She taught the girls; I taught the boys. I had come to know and respect Barbara for her wisdom and godly character. And she was a straight shooter with her words too. I asked for Barbara's advice about what to do. Should I follow through and accept the position, leaving my family and fiancé behind. (We would still get married, but that was still ten months away and Pam would have to do most of the preparation herself while I was out of state.)

Barbara's advice to me that day was, "You already know what to do George. Pray. You've got to pray about it and listen for God's answer. Listen for God's answer as you read your Bible in your regular study." Then she said, "I will be praying too." She was right. I did know to pray and seek God's answer. I guess, I just needed to hear from someone else, someone God had put in my life for that very reason.

After hanging up the phone and before going into work that afternoon, I picked up my Bible study material to begin preparing for the upcoming Sunday School lesson for my junior high boys. The lesson for the coming week was Scripture from 1 Samuel chapters 1 and 2.

It is the story of Hannah, who had no children but desperately wanted to give her husband children. In desperation, one day she found herself on the temple steps praying aloud, wailing and crying out to God to open her womb and give her a child. So desperate was she that she promised God if He would give her a son, she would dedicate the child back to Him for life. Not only dedicate Him to the Lord but give him to be raised by the priest in the temple, serving God. God blessed her with a son within the year, and after she weaned him, she gave him over to be raised in the temple.

As I read that Scripture passage that morning, God showed me that giving up something that I loved and treasured (family, fiancé, and my church home) for a time in order to follow Him would prove much greater in value than staying close to family. It was clear.

God's desire for me was made evident with the first reading of that passage for the week. I thought I picked up my Bible and materials to study for my students. But God's plan was to speak into my life that morning. His plan had bccn in process long before that morning.

That lesson plan had been written well over a year earlier and printed for that particular week more than thirteen months prior. God knew in advance and was prepared well ahead of time for what I needed that day.

I had my answer. I knew what I was to do. I followed my calling. But not before making a call myself. To Barbara Wooden. She's the first one I had to share this good news with — and to thank her for her prayers and guidance. Then I shared it with my fiancé, my family, and later, my church family.

I discovered that day that to find God's answer, you do not go looking for Scripture to give you God's answer. Instead, you read a portion each day and watch God give you His answer as you read through your regular reading plan. If you go looking through Scripture for a particular passage that fits your thinking, you will surely miss God's answer.

God moved me to Ohio while working in the corporate world so He could position and align me with the right people to later call me into full-time ordained ministry. The years in between, God had me with a company that poured into me and built my leadership abilities. He has since used those abilities and continues to use them in ways that still amaze me. We serve a great God. I have found there is no greater pleasure or satisfaction than following God's calling.

Thus far, it has been an amazing journey that I could not have imagined that morning thirty-five-plus years ago.

Jehovah-Jireh, God is my provider!

Hired Beyond Human Expectation

How did you get hired? I was asked this question by a corporate recruiter three to four months after he interviewed and hired me into a management position with the second largest hard-lines retailer of its kind in the nation. My only response to him was, "You hired me." It was true. After going through the interview and testing process this man assisted in the final decision. So why did I find myself sitting in an office across from this man from the corporate office being asked this question?

The tone of his voice had declared he was not second guessing his decision. I was not underperforming. In fact, I was moving through the management training program at an accelerated pace. His response to me when I said, "You hired me," was, "I know I did. But you cannot get into the management training program with us without a college degree or coming up through the ranks of one of our stores." I knew this from the interviewing process and was surprised when I had received the call that the job was mine if I desired.

He went on to say, "You have neither. So how did you get hired?" He said it with a slight smile. I believe he knew as well as I did at that moment that this was a God-thing. Somehow God had blinded this man and other decision-makers through the interviewing process — blinded them to the company policy and my lack of meeting those requirements.

The management training course was a ten- to twelve- month process. I completed it in less than six months and was in a store supervising the sales floor and operations. During my seven-year tenure with that company, God blessed me tremendously and grew me greatly. The training this company provided for its leadership was second to none in the western hemisphere. It was so good, in fact, that other companies were continuously stealing away this company's leaders with higher pay, benefits, and other incentives. God would later show me why He had me there for those seven years.

Retail management is very demanding on your time. I often worked eighty- to one hundred-plus hours a week while also serving as youth minister for a growing church. At one point, my wife and I began praying for God to move me out of that company and into a position where I could better serve Him. Instead of moving me out, God moved my supervisor out. He accepted a position at the company's main offices. He was not a bad or evil man, though his actions sometimes seemed a little vindictive or spiteful.

We were relieved at his transfer, but not certain what the next supervisor would be like.

While sitting in my office one morning, I saw my new supervisor for the first time as he entered the hallway carrying a box into the empty office across the hall from mine. I went over to introduce myself and as soon as I said my name, he turned to me and said, "I hear you like to go to church. From now on when it is your Sunday to work, you come in after church." Wow! What a change from the man who previously occupied this office. It was at that moment that I realized God was telling me He had heard our prayers. And He was clearly telling me that He was not finished with me yet at this company.

Through the next five years, I was able to see the hand of God at work with opportunities to share my Christian walk and Scripture, as well as counsel others and lead some to faith in Christ. At one point, a discussion arose among the salespeople and other employees as to what was the unpardonable sin. Apparently after some time of discussion around the breakroom table, a couple of employees came to me and I was able to write a two-page paper on the topic (sharing the gospel in the midst) and gave it to be distributed amongst the employees who desired to read it. God at work!

About three years after I left the company and was serving full time in ministry at a local church, my path crossed with one of my former employees. This young man had been a good employee for a couple of years until one day he used bad judgment. I terminated this employee for theft. But now some five years later when we met again, he told of his current life situation, including his engagement. Then he asked if I would perform the marriage ceremony. This man who I had terminated — who I had fired — was asking me to perform his wedding ceremony. God at work! I agreed and during our second premarital counseling session, he and his fiancé accepted Christ as the personal Lord and Savior of their lives. They began a new walk together as one and one with the Lord.

The book of Exodus tells us that Moses and the recently freed Israelite nation were standing at the edge of the Red Sea with the Egyptian army of more than 600 chariots coming to capture and kill them. The Israelites had no place to go, no place to run. Moses declared to the Israelites, "Do not be afraid. Stand still, and see the salvation of the LORD, which He will accomplish for you today. For the Egyptians whom you see today, you shall see again no more forever. The LORD will fight for you, and you shall hold your peace" (Ex. 14:13-14, NKJV).

You likely know the story. (If not, look it up and read this miraculous account.) Moses raised his hands over the edge of waters and God parted the sea so that all the Israelite nation crossed over on dry land. No mud, no puddles, completely dry. After they had crossed over to the other side and the Egyptian army came into the ocean bed, the waters flowed back into the ocean drowning the entire army, never to be seen again, just as God had promised. Sometimes life looks like a dead end, but there are no dead ends with God.

You never know how or when God is going to use you. Don't close the door because you want something better or because you do not believe that you belong. God has far greater vision than you or I. Keep praying and keep your eyes on God. He will lead you into opportunities that you never dreamed possible. So when a question comes to you similar to, "How did you get hired?" don't fight it. Instead, smile, look up and say, "I'm ready Lord. Let's do this Your way!"

Jehovah-Jireh, God is my provider!

My Father's Hand

In my early thirties, our church had a revival. I served as a volunteer in the youth ministry at the church. During the revival, three of my friends and ministry coworkers plus several others made decisions to follow Christ. Each had made a public commitment earlier in life (as had I), but now each one was stating that the first one was not genuine or whole. When several people you know, trust, and watch live what appear to be godly lives make this decision in a matter of a few days, you might begin to scratch your head and question your own salvation. I did.

I remember getting alone with God and asking, "God, is that me too? Do I need to make that decision?" In that unmistakable voice that God sometimes uses — not audible, but just as clear and distinct — came His reply. It was three simple words: "Don't you remember?"

With those three words my heart was settled as a rush of refreshing comfort washed over me. The entire scene flashed before me in that split second and I had my answer. The scene that flashed as quickly as those three words was this:

My family of seven sat in pretty much the same place every Sunday morning in worship. On this particular Sunday, my oldest brother Bill, who was twelve years old, was sitting next to the aisle to my right. At nine years of age, I was seated next to him. My dad was to my left, my mother on his left and then my sister and second oldest brother to Mom's left. And my youngest brother, Jim, was asleep in my dad's arms. The time in the service came when the invitation was given to respond to God's speaking in our personal lives. Customarily, in our denomination, when the invitation was given, if you felt led by the Holy Spirit, you walked down the aisle and told the preacher what God desired of you that morning.

On this Sunday morning, I knew it was time for me to go to the front and speak to the pastor about surrendering my life to God, inviting Jesus to be my Lord and Savior. Honestly, I could feel this strange sensation moving inside me and somehow I knew it was God. I did not know all the answers or all the details. I just knew I was supposed to go down and talk to the pastor about it. And I knew without a doubt God was directing those impulses.

I was a very shy, bashful young boy. When I first felt God stirring me, I looked to my older brother. I knew if I could get his attention, he would go with me. After all, he had made this walk and this decision before in his own life. He would be there for me. Unfortunately, I could not get his attention and I dared not make a scene. That was forbidden in our family. Next, I turned to my dad. I was nine and he was my dad. He was invincible and the strong tower I needed. Certainly, he would understand and would walk with me. But when I looked up at him towering above me with my two-year-old brother asleep on his shoulder, Dad could not see me. He was turned forward, focused, and singing.

I looked back to my brother. Still unable to get his attention and knowing I was being compelled to step out into the aisle before it was too late, I pressed around him and stepped out to make that walk alone. It was scary for a bashful, skinny nine-year-old boy. I knew I was doing what God desired of me, but I was still terrified of walking in front of all those people and talking to the preacher. But I did it. I stepped out into the aisle. That is when it happened. This is what God was reminding me of twenty-plus years later.

Once in the aisle, before my second foot hit the ground, I felt my Father's hand across my back resting on my right shoulder. An unexplainable sense of relief covered my entire body as soon as I felt my Father's hand. I had known he would be with me. What a relief the touch of his hand was to this frightened little boy. I looked up over my left shoulder to show my relief and gratefulness for Him realizing what was happening and walking with me.

Only, when I looked up over my shoulder, my dad was still in the same place, with my brother asleep in his arms. He had not moved. Talk about shock! But the shock was immediately wiped away. Realizing the hand on my shoulder was real and I was in the aisle by myself, I knew right then and there that while my dad and brother were still in place, I knew my Father — my Heavenly Father — was in the aisle with me. And He would match me step for step. The impression of the touch of His hand on my shoulder was so real it was the confirmation that He was with me and He would never leave or forsake me.

As I write this, and every time I get to share it, I remember His hand on my shoulder. It was God's hand of compassion and redemption. And it is as if I can feel it each time. Even better yet, He truly has never walked away or forsaken me. Even when I turned away from Him. So, on that day, twenty-plus years later, in my early thirties, while I had been serving God faithfully for several years, a renewed resolve began in my life. I never want to be without the touch of His hand on my shoulder and my life.

If you have never experienced the comforting touch of the God of all creation it is not too late.

Grab a Bible, begin reading the book titled The Gospel of John in the New Testament and call out to God to reveal himself to you. Your experience will be different from mine. God is a personal God and He desires to have an individually unique experience with you. Afterwards, contact a pastor, preacher or reach out to me. I'd love to rejoice with you.

Jehovah-Jireh, God is my provider!

Aerobics in the Church?

Beth arrived at my office in the church for a scheduled appointment. She was confident in the topic of discussion. Two years earlier, I approached one of the young ladies in our church, an aerobics instructor, about the possibility of starting an aerobics ministry at the church. A godly, Christian mother and wife in our church, she would be doing in the church what she was already doing at the community recreation center — only with Christian music and a devotion each session. But then, she informed me that her husband had taken a job in another state. They would be moving. I accepted that as a closed door from God. I did not try to find another person to start that ministry.

Now, two years later, Beth had contacted me and was sitting in my office to talk about something she believed God had laid on her heart. Beth held seven different certifications in aerobics instruction, CPR and first aid. Yet, she admitted to herself that she was a little nervous, maybe even anxious. While aerobics was her passion, this would be a different undertaking. Beth had approached me a week earlier and scheduled an appointment to speak about a ministry possibility she was interested in and believed God was leading her to undertake.

After exchanging greetings, I voiced a prayer for our meeting and the possibility of reaching people for Christ with a new ministry. As the discussion progressed Beth stated her desire to combine two of her passions: aerobics and sharing about God. Beth was leading several aerobics classes at the local community recreation center and was a well-respected, and likeable person. She was grateful for being able to work in an area she was so passionate about.

But for Beth something was missing.

"A few months ago, driving home after leading classes at the rec center, I felt as though God were asking me when I was going to do this for Him," she shared. "I thought I was doing it for God. And I was. But God was asking me to take it a step farther. God wanted me to combine my passion and ability as an aerobics instructor with sharing the gospel. I just wasn't sure how."

Following that discussion with God in her car, Beth began a journey of discovery. The idea God planted in her heart and mind that day became almost an obsession.

Beth confessed, "I was thinking about it all the time. When I woke up in the morning, around the house, during classes, after class, driving, during meals, even here at church during the sermon. I cannot help it. It is always there, on my mind."

I smiled and gave a nod of understanding — actually I was bubbling over inside. This is the type of disciple-making ministry we had been teaching and preaching about. Believers finding their passion and combining it with a zeal to fulfill the Great Commission — to make disciples. Then I asked Beth this question: "What do you think God is leading you to do with all this?"

Beth moved forward in her chair (a sign of assurance) and with excitement in her voice began, "I believe God wants me to teach Christian aerobics. And I really want to do it here at the church. I would use Christian music, pray at the beginning and end of every class, and share a devotion. And I would want to open it up to the community, not just the ladies at our church."

The discussion continued for about twenty-five minutes. I then summarized what Beth and I had discussed for the next steps of ministry.

"So you are going to go home and write a ministry plan for this. In that plan you are going to state what the ministry will be, the objective of the ministry, and how you will use it as a disciple-making ministry helping fulfill the Great Commission?"

We agreed and closed the meeting by praying for Beth and thanking God for laying this opportunity on her heart and asking for His guidance for Beth as she wrote the ministry plan. We moved forward with God's desire.

Beth returned two weeks later with her two-year old daughter in tow and presented the ministry plan. We read and reviewed the plan together (with a few small, two-year old, interruptions).

"This is good. You did a good job, Beth. I look forward to seeing how God uses this and you to further His kingdom work. Be sure to stick to His plan."

I was excited for Beth and this ministry opportunity, though I knew that I was the one who would have to answer the critics and dispute any claims of this not being a biblical ministry. Yet, knowing the quality of Beth's spiritual life and spending time with her in these two meetings, I also knew this was a God-given opportunity.

Somewhat surprisingly, there was very little rebuttal and no kick-back from the congregation at all. The very first night Beth had close to twenty women in attendance, two from outside the church. The next week the numbers grew and four women from outside the church joined the class. Within the first year, not only were women getting in shape, but they were also learning about God, and at least one of those ladies accepted Christ as Lord and Savior. And two became regular attendees in worship services — as well as the aerobics class.

God knew two years earlier what he had in mind for Beth and our church facility. He planted the thought in my heart, then let it lay dormant for two years until His timing was right for Beth, the church, and the community. God is so much greater than good. His ways, His timing is always right.

God and Beth played the major roles in this. I only facilitated the discussions with Beth, prompting her with the right types of questions, and creating a path of planning and implementation. Writing the ministry plan afforded Beth and church leaders a plan of action and concrete goals. At the first meeting, I knew if this was not from God and not a true passion, Beth would not be able to complete the ministry plan in an efficient manner.

But not just the written plan. More importantly, the implementation and fruit of the ministry solidified the God-given passion of Beth's for this ministry — a disciple-making ministry.

Jehovah-Jireh, God is my provider!

New Ministries

The fruitfulness of the aerobics ministry in the previous entry led to the account I am about to relate to you. A young man in our church, probably in his thirties, approached me in the hallway one Sunday a few months after the launch of the aerobics ministry. Let's call him Carl. Carl was a former military man. Apparently, in the military he learned and taught a form of martial arts. Hearing of the fruitfulness of the aerobics ministry, Carl stated that he wanted to teach this martial arts discipline in our church.

I have nothing against martial arts or Carl, and certainly nothing against new ministries to bring people to the saving grace of Christ and building disciples. In fact, due to the disciplines of martial arts, I could envision a fruitful disciple-growing ministry. However, after talking with Carl in the hallway for only a couple short minutes on this day, I knew where this was going.

Much like the young lady with the aerobics ministry, I asked Carl to call the office and set an appointment so we could discuss this ministry possibility and I could share with him about writing a ministry plan. I stated that he would need to put a ministry plan into writing. His facial expression and body language revealed something to me right then and I knew it was not likely that he would follow through. Unlike the young lady with the aerobics ministry, I never heard from Carl again about the martial arts ministry. This did not surprise me. Why?

In the brief encounter in the hallway, I could tell by Carl's demeanor that he was serious, thinking this could be a great ministry opportunity — and I agree that it could have been. I could also tell by his delivery and demeanor that this would unfortunately be a fleeting moment for Carl. While a worthy and noble pursuit, his passion would wane and die away. The truth is, I am not certain there was ever any God-given passion in Carl's heart for this as a ministry. But I was willing to follow God's lead.

Starting new ministries in the church is a great way to advance the Kingdom of God — if those ministries are God-sent and God-ordained. Too often in churches we hear or read of something another church is doing and we try to bring that to our church. This is copying models. Copying models is never in our best interest. My mantra is, "Don't copy models, capture principles." What are the biblical principles making that a successful and fruitful ministry for that church? Then look at the particular giftings in your church and determine how you can use your giftings with those principles.

Each year, God has provided many wonderful opportunities for new ministries in and through the local church. Yet, we must open our eyes to things we have been closed to in years past. We must be ready and willing to follow God in His desire to be His Church, not the church of our comfort. Regardless of past successes or shortcomings, we must be willing to let go of the grip we have on what we believe the church is. New ministries and new processes abound and are likely to be the church of the future. In many aspects, this church of the future — if it is to be fruitful — will look more like the church found in the book of Acts than what we have called church for the last century.

Attached are links to two free resources every church can use for greater impact in ministry as we move forward.

One is a ministry evaluation form. I believe every church should evaluate each ministry every year. You are not going to do away with all ministries but evaluate them for fruitfulness. What functions of the church are being fulfilled? Which parts of the Great Commission have been fulfilled this past year through this ministry?

The other resource is a New Ministry questionnaire. Eighteen questions to answer before starting any new ministry or event in your church. Both of these resources can be vital to the success of your ministry service to God.

New Ministry Questionnaire – https://soncare.net/wp-content/uploads/2020/09/New-Ministry-Questionnaire.pdf

Ministry Evaluation - https://soncare.net/wp-content/uploads/2018/06/Evaluating-Ministries.pdf

New ministries can be very fruitful for building God's Kingdom. However, if they are man's ideas and not from God, like Carl's martial arts ministry idea, it will likely fade away. Carl's idea of a martial arts ministry had great potential; it just was not from God for that church at that time. Starting new ministries for the sake of starting something new is not God's way. Starting a new ministry because it sounds fun, easy, or comfortable is not a God-driven ministry. Ministry is doing for others, but God's ministry requires commitment, dedication, and labor.

What is the biggest hurdle for your church in beginning viable, God-sent ministries to reach your community? What ministry opportunities has God placed before you in the past 30 days that your church could respond to, answering the eighteen questions on the new ministry form?

Jehovah-Jireh, God will provide!

Being Taught About Teaching

*T*aching *That Bears Fruit*, my first book, was published in 2001. There were several "God-moments" in developing, writing, and launching that book. One such moment happened at night in my little teal green worship center on wheels. I had several great worship experiences driving along in that truck.

But let me backup because this story begins prior to my experience that night.

I had been working for several months on my first book. The working title had been *Teaching to Change Lives*. I had sent it to a few publishers with that working title and was coming close to the time to choose the right publisher for this work.

It was during this selection phase that I discovered that Howard Hendricks, a well-known Christian education author had recently published a book with the same title.

"Great! I can't compete with Howard Hendricks," I thought. "Now what?"

In my ponderings, I talked with a fellow minister and colleague of mine, Barry Dollar. Barry had left the corporate world as a well-paid graphic designer to follow God in ministry. His advice was right on target.

"Play with the words in the title," he said. "Rearrange them. See what works, what seems right."

Then he went on to give me a couple suggestions. "*Changing Lives Through Teaching.* Or *Life Changing Teaching.*" He stated.

Throughout the day, I followed Barry's suggestion. Nothing seemed to fall into place, but I didn't reject any either. I rearranged the words "Teaching to Change Lives" every way I could think. Sometimes injecting a new word into the equation. No staggering revelations came that long day at the office.

Daylight had disappeared into darkness by the time I left the church that evening for my twenty-five-minute drive home. Listening to Christian music on the radio and talking with God about other things as I drove, I was having a pleasant unwinding drive that evening. Then, out of nowhere, a picture appeared in my head and four words covered part of the photo. At the same moment a sense of joy and relief overcame my entire being. So strong was this impression and sensation that I quickly pulled into a shopping center parking lot. So quickly that if anyone had been behind or beside me, there would've been a collision. Thankfully, God was in control of this whole experience.

I pulled over for two distinct reasons. One, to completely be engulfed by the wonderfully overwhelming sensation I was experiencing, and two, to call Barry Dollar. I had to share this with someone right then, and since Barry had been in my office early that morning giving me the idea, I knew it had to be Barry.

Already home for the evening, Barry answered his phone and with no other introduction I said, "Barry, picture this. A fully green tree heavy laden with fresh fruit and emblazoned across the front of it the words: *Teaching That Bears Fruit.*"

After a noticeably short pause, Barry said, "I think you've got it."

To which I enthusiastically replied (as if I was not already enthusiastic enough), "No! I know I've got it! God gave that to me."

Then I went on explaining about how it had all unfolded that evening. How I had let go and was not talking to God about the title, just worshipping Him in my truck. That is when He revealed to me the title of the book.

If the story ended there, it would be remarkable enough. God had shown up and delivered a truly divine experience that evening. But God was not finished at only one revelation that evening.

I arrived at the office the next morning as usual, my normal time. I walked past Barry's office to get to mine. Barry was already at his desk working. Since he had school-aged children, most days he arrived after me. I walked into my office and began putting things away from the work meetings and discipleship programs the previous day.

It was at least five minutes before I sat down at my desk and turned on my computer screen. When I did, I let out a hallelujah cry of joy and adulation. Within a couple seconds, Barry was standing at my office door with a big grin on his face.

Remember how I said God was not finished at only one revelation the previous evening? After my phone call the night before, God put an impression on Barry's mind. When I turned my computer on that morning the only thing on the screen was a picture of a variety of fresh fruit, some sliced, some whole on a neutral gray background. Above the fruit, in block letters were the words, "Teaching That Bears Fruit."

Barry had stayed up late, into the wee hours of the morning, designing what would become the front cover of *Teaching That Bears Fruit.* Not because he had to, but because of the conviction in my voice the night before and God's impression on Barry's heart. Then after being up late, he intentionally arrived early at the office and uploaded the photo to my computer so it would be there to surprise me when I arrived.

We laughed later that he had been sitting in his office waiting to hear my reaction, but nothing came. He waited and waited unaware that I was tending to other things tidying up my office.

He said, "I was wondering what was happening. Did it not come on? Did George not like it? Had he not seen it?"

But when my shout of joy went up, he was elated as well and came to celebrate. That cover still dawns the front of God's first book through me, *Teaching That Bears Fruit*.

God's ways and His thoughts are far greater than mine. His timing is always perfect. And He knows the right people to use in every situation. God gave me the title in my worship experience that evening when I least expected it. He gave Barry the vision for the book cover.

"'For My thoughts are not your thoughts, and your ways are not My ways.' This is the LORD's declaration. 'For as heaven is higher than earth, so My ways are higher than your ways, and My thoughts than your thoughts.'" (Isaiah 55:8-9).

Jehovah-Jireh, God is my provider!

Trust Through a House Break-in & Robbery

It was a calm, cool November evening as my wife, Pam, and I walked out the door of our home for the thirty-minute drive to church for dinner and a meeting. We walked out, locked the front door and headed to the car. On the sidewalk a few steps from the front door, I stopped, turned back toward the house. I hesitated for a couple of seconds contemplating if I should go back in and leave the front room light on as we usually do when we return home after dark. Time was limited, and I was the main speaker for the evening. So I chose not to unlock the door, go in, and turn the light on. We walked to the car and drove off towards the city.

We returned that evening in the dark, in a good mood following a nice evening with church family. I unlocked the front door, turned on the light, and proceeded down the hallway toward the bedrooms. I stopped first at my office, flipped the light switch to an unfamiliar sight. Papers everywhere. Closet doors open, bags and boxes strewn open across the floor.

I called to my wife, "Stay where you are."

"What?" she said as she started down the hallway.

"Go back, stay there. We've been robbed," I called out.

I turned on the light in our bedroom. Every drawer but one in the dresser and all drawers in the wardrobe were emptied on the floor, contents scattered in small piles. The mattress and box springs were flipped up. Our heavy mirror had been pulled a foot away from the wall.

I made my way back to the other end of the house. One thing stood out immediately: the wires from the TV were laying bare where our VCR used to sit. That night, we lost my wife's jewelry box and her jewelry, my valet box — given as a goodbye gift from fellow hospital employees — which contained my grandfather's pocket watch, my deceased father's pen set, my high school ring, and other sentimental keepsakes. In addition, about $3,500 worth of camera equipment had been stolen, and one gym duffel bag and a pillowcase, apparently to carry their loot in.

But the $5,000 claim and the damage to one window and the back door paled in comparison to the mental and emotional loss that night. It would be a week before my wife would sleep in our bedroom again. We slept on the hide-a-bed sofa with the lights on in our living room. We also had an alarm system installed and extra security lights. Still, the theft of peace of mind and safety in our own home prevailed.

The feeling of personal violation and loss of security would linger long after receiving a compensation check for the lost and damaged material possessions from our insurance company.

There are many lessons learned from God through this experience. One of the most important was trust. While our lives were invaded and our peace of mind violated, our trust in God and His people was invigorated and strengthened.

I do not know how late it was that evening when I called our neighbors who lived about one hundred yards away past a wooded lot. Russell and Linda were great neighbors in our rural community. A godly man and woman who did not hesitate to help when called. They sat with us, prayed with us and stayed long after the police left. Then, Linda sat with Pam while Russell and I worked to board up the broken window and repair the door enough to close and lock. Then, they stayed a while longer and checked on us again the next morning. In addition to our neighbors, our church family supported us in many ways as well.

God's people unite and serve one another in each other's time of need. This is biblical community. This is what is demonstrated in the book of Acts and throughout the Bible.

"Now all the believers were together and held all things in common. They sold their possessions and property and distributed the proceeds to all, as anyone had a need. Every day they devoted themselves to meeting together in the temple complex, and broke bread from house to house. They ate their food with a joyful and humble attitude, praising God and having favor with all the people. And every day the Lord added to them those who were being saved." (Acts 2:44-47).

Russell Lamb has since gone on to his heavenly reward, but I will never forget not only this November night in 1994, but all the times Russell and Linda proved to be God's servants – perhaps His angels unaware. While we live several hundred miles and states apart today, I believe to this day, twenty-five years later, if I called on Linda, she would respond as best she could. And I trust she knows Pam and I would be there for her as well.

One lesson learned: Even in trials and personal violation, God and His servants can be trusted to sit and walk with you. God has individuals in your life whom you can trust to be there for you through the trials.

"Be not forgetful to entertain strangers: for thereby some have entertained angels unawares" (Heb. 13:2, KJV). Not only strangers, but your neighbors too!

Jehovah-Jireh, God is my provider!

I Surrender All

On my way to my Sunday Bible study class, where I taught teenagers, my pastor asked me to step into his office.

Now, this is not like getting called into the principal's office. I had chaired the committee that brought this pastor to the church — under God's direction and calling.

During that time or since, I had not spoken to the pastor about my (and my wife's) sensing God's call into full-time ministry. We had been praying about it for more than two years by this time, though no one at the church knew. I was very committed to and passionate about student ministry.

In his office that morning, the major question asked was, "Would you pray about working in the adults and education ministry within the church?"

Before I could begin my answer, which was going to start with my passion for youth ministry, he held up one hand stopping me, then interjected, "I know you have a passion for youth ministry, but would you consider praying about it?"

What was I going to say to my pastor? "Absolutely not"?

Of course I was willing to pray for God's answer. Even back then I knew enough to realize God's plans are much better than mine. Along with accepting this ministry position, also I would be accepting God's call into full-time ministry.

While Pam and I had been praying for more than two years for God's direction, I had always expected it would be in student ministry. After all, that's what I knew and loved. Surely it would be that or at least use my corporate leadership experience in a para-church organization — one that works alongside churches assisting them in accomplishing their mission.

In praying about the decision of accepting the call to full-time ministry, I wanted Pam to ask God to take her to a new level in her spiritual walk. Shortly after that meeting, on the way home from church one Sunday evening, I talked with her about asking God to reveal His will to her through Scripture. She had never experienced this before.

"You never go looking for the answer," I explained. "Rather, you wait and listen for God to speak through your daily reading in His word."

Every Tuesday morning at 6:30, I met with three other gentlemen. We all served in the youth ministry of our church. Two days after my conversation with Pam, one of the men handed each of us a copy of a magazine article. The first part of the article was about how churched teens were not much more spiritual than their unchurched friends. I thought, God, is this your answer? Am I to stay in youth ministry helping these teens?

Then as I turned to the second page the first sentence of the second paragraph read, "You reach the kids by reaching their fathers."

In that very second God spoke to me, "This is why I've called you into ministry."

You reach the children by reaching their parents. As I read that article, God clearly spoke, showing me the full-time adult and education ministry position in front of me was His will. I had God's answer.

When I got home that evening, Pam met me at the door, excited. Pam never greets me at the door. It was a June Cleaver moment.

With excitement in her voice, she said, "I've got to show you something." And with that she disappeared down the hall.

I knew one of two things had happened: either Publishers Clearing House had dropped off a check for ten million dollars or the Fashion Shop had a big sale that day. Why else would she meet me at the door so excited?

She returned a minute later, not with a big mock check and not with a handful of dresses, but with her Bible in hand. We sat down on the couch in the front room and she opened her Bible to 1 Timothy. She explained she had finished reading a book in the Old Testament and that morning turned to 1 Timothy, without reason, to read next. Then she read aloud to me verse 12 of chapter one: "And I thank Christ Jesus, our Lord, who has enabled me, and found me trustworthy appointing me to ministry."

She said, "When I read that verse, God said, 'This is why I have called George into the ministry.' "

Don't miss this folks. God spoke to two people in the same half hour, 25 miles apart, in two different ways using the same wording to confirm His calling on my life.

We had been praying for God's direction into full-time ministry. But this was not what I had expected. And it certainly has not been the ride I expected. But man, what an amazing ride it has been, far exceeding my expectations.

Do not be afraid of tomorrow or the changes it may bring. Embrace the change that God brings into your life and look diligently into how you are to join Him in His work. It may very well look different than you expect. You know what I say to that? Praise God, bring it on!

Life is not about coincidence. It is about God in my circumstances. It is about me joining God in what He is already doing in the circumstances I find myself in. Joining God in His work brings the greatest joy and satisfaction that can be had on earth.

Jehovah-Jireh, God is my provider!

The Importance of a Devotion —
Be Still and Know

I t was in the early morning on a typical summer's day in June 1993. I started the day like most days. One of the first things on my agenda, even before my shower, is to spend some alone time with God — a quiet time of devotion, Scripture reading and prayer for my part in the day ahead of me. Only this devotion would be different, special.

Less than four weeks prior to this morning, I had attended a meeting of all the operations managers in the east region of the retail company that I worked for. Still in my thirties, as I looked around the room, I noticed everyone was new, and younger than myself and one other operations manager, Bob. Not one of them had been with the company for six months. Bob had supervised part of my training. During a morning break, I queried Bob about what I noticed. He concurred. He had noticed the same thing. Then he began apprising me of what he knew and what had been happening at his store, to him personally.

Things at his store were changing. He was suddenly being treated differently by his general manager and the district manager. He began explaining peculiar attitudes and evaluations, work schedule changes, and increased expectations that were not normal or reasonable. Bob said it was as if they were intentionally trying to make working life difficult for Bob, who had been an exemplary operations manager. So good, in fact, that he had trained several other operations managers over the years, including me.

Then Bob began telling me of conversations he'd had with some of our former colleagues. They had listed the same steps within similar timeframes prior to their dismissal from the company. It was evident the company was realigning their leadership strategy according to the recommendations from a capital acquisition and consulting firm. It would be odd for 43 operations managers in stores from six or seven states to suddenly begin failing in areas they had been commended for in prior years. So instead of all at once, when one or two were dismissed from the company, the same routine would begin for a few others.

As Bob spoke that day, I recognized something about my own situation. The exact same steps were happening to me. At least the first two. I was about four months behind Bob in the process. Bob was let go from the company within a couple of weeks.

Following that meeting and Bob's dismissal, people from other stores were calling our store, speaking to me or the sales manager with dates on when my termination would come. Not because they thought I had it coming. Just the opposite, in fact, they could see what the company was doing. The company had a process of elimination. Most everyone's prediction was within two weeks of the day I was dismissed. I was the last of my generation of operations managers to be let go.

Three months after my termination, all of the forty-three general managers in our region were let go in one day. They had been instructed on the process for terminating the operations managers' employment, then they were all dismissed in one day.

In one city, all the store managers were called away from the store to a hotel under the pretense of a general manager's meeting. Once at the hotel, they were asked to surrender their store keys and other company items. They were then told to go home and not to return to the store. Their personal belongings would be shipped to them from their store office. Talk about weird. But it is reality.

My termination came in September. So, why did I stay for almost four months knowing what was going to happen? It all comes back to my devotion time on this June morning. My Scripture reading included 2 Chronicles 20:17: "You will not need to fight in this battle. Position yourselves, stand still and see the salvation of the Lord, who is with you."

The very moment I read those words I felt a rush over me. A complete wave of release washed through my body, starting in the hairs on my head extending all the way to my toes. I had never before experienced that same God-sent sensation — and I have not since. It was God, through His Living Word, and the Holy Spirit washing over me, cleansing my mind, body, and spirit of the tension, stress, and angst of the situation.

For the next three and a half months, I went to work and carried out my duties as I had every day prior. There was nothing I could do about the situation except stand still and watch the salvation of the Lord. The peace I received that June morning remained with me through those trying times and continued afterward. Though when the day came and my general and district managers asked to speak with me, I knew what was coming and my nervous system went berserk.

I had brought closure to the ordeal and moved on. Then one day, five years later in September, I saw my former district manager, both of us shopping at one of the competitor stores.

I was congenial to him and he told me he had been terminated from our former company. He began to share how they let him go. The steps he described sounded so familiar. I do not believe he recognized that the strategy used to dismiss him was the same strategy he had been taught to use on me and the others. It was exactly the same.

After hearing his story, on the walk through the parking lot to my car, God asked me what day it was. I reflected on it and realized it was five years, exactly, to the date that man had terminated me. God, at that moment, completed the promise He gave me in my devotion five years and four months earlier: "You will not need to fight in this battle. Position yourselves, stand still and see the salvation of the Lord, who is with you."

I stayed true to my job in the store during the four months, and stayed true to God and trusted His promises. I did not need that confirmation five years later, but God wanted to remind me one more time. He is faithful and just. God does keep His promises.

Jehovah-Jireh, God is my provider!

Six Figure Experience

For a year and a half after being let go from the second largest retailer of its kind in the nation, I was a sojourner, a wanderer awaiting God's call. I took a job and kept it for a few months working for a sweepstakes sales company. Then an opportunity came along to manage the opening of a hardlines retail mall store. It was to be a trial run during the fall and Christmas season. If the store did well, the company would likely keep it open.

I had no desire of staying in retail management but God provided the opportunity, it was certainly within my field of experience, and it paid the bills. The Christmas season was a success. The company signed a long-term lease with the mall and walls were built to replace curtains separating the sales floor from the back stock room.

I would run that store for another six months. During this time, I had opportunities to leave for other retailers. One day, a friend of mine called. I had trained this man in his first sales endeavor over a dozen years earlier. Now, he was the lead trainer for the largest flooring retailer in the nation. He was coming to Cincinnati from their corporate offices in Dallas, Texas, and wanted to meet with me. I was happy to make the thirty-minute drive to meet with him and catch up on his career.

His intention for the meeting was more than I expected. He was there to offer me a position — a corner office position in their corporate headquarters with a six-figure income. That's hard to pass up.

At the mall a couple of weeks later, a lady who managed another hardlines retail store stopped me outside her store. We had become friends managing stores inside the same mall and we learned of each other's history. This day her conversation was different from other days.

She said, "I've been asked to ask you to come to work for us. We know who you are, and we know what you've done (meaning my experience in the retail industry). You can have your choice..." She named a position in their corporate offices, then stated, "Or we'll create a position for you. You name it." All of that was spectacular. Then, after a short pause she added, "Oh, and I was told to tell you money is not an obstacle."

Wow! What in the world was happening? I am not special, nor would I ever consider myself specially gifted. Two six-figure income offers within weeks of each other. This one was basically offering for me to write my own ticket and determine my own income.

What did I do? Which of these exceptional offers did I accept? Neither one.

I thanked both people for the great opportunities, but stated, "I'm already talking with someone else."

That someone else was God. My belief was God was going to use me in some other line of work, most likely ministry. While He had not revealed that assignment to me yet, God was working in my heart and life, sometimes in ways I was not even aware of.

My true belief was that God would place me in church ministry since I had been serving as bivocational youth minister for a few years. My other thought was it might be with some para-church organization.

Wherever it would be though, there would not be anywhere near a six-figure income. Perhaps this was God testing me, strengthening my faithfulness in Him. Would I go for the money or trust God with providing for me?

It was not long until God opened the door to a full-time ministry position in a local church. The income for that ministry position was far less than a six-figure income. It was even quite a bit less than I was making before being let go from the retailer one and a half years earlier.

I served that church for five years. When we left to follow God's call to a church in another state, we had more money in the bank than ever. We never missed a payment or meal. All on a significantly less income than we had previously.

God truly blessed us and showed us that He truly is Jehovah-Jireh, my provider.

But not only financially, let's be clear. God provided a place for me to exercise the leadership experience I had been given in retail. He also provided great, lifelong relationships, spiritual strengthening and maturity, experience assisting other churches, and the joy and satisfaction that only comes from God. No six-figure income could come close to God's provision!

I served on church staff for several years, then as a denominational worker assisting about one hundred churches. Within my first year in full-time church ministry, God brought people into my life who called on me to lead conferences and train others in ministry. In every place I served on church and denominational staff through the years, God has used me to influence, encourage, and pour into the lives of other ministry leaders.

About six paragraphs above, I shared that I believed God was going to use me in either church ministry or para-church service. Well, you can insert a smiley face right here because He has blessed me to do both! May He continue to use me to pour into others as others pour into me daily, and may I be found faithful at every turn.

Jehovah-Jireh, God is my provider!

A Sunday Night Phone Call

On a Sunday evening voice message I heard, "I'll be in my car for the next four hours. Give me a call when you get this message."

I received this voice message when my wife and I returned home from the church I was serving one Sunday evening. The call came from a friend of mine, Terry Herald.

Terry had served as pastor of our church in Ohio for two years. I had served on the search committee that brought him to our church and was later invited to join the church staff. Terry was now serving in Huntsville, Alabama.

Shortly after hearing the message, I called my friend on his car phone. After exchanging greetings, Terry stated the reason for his call: "I don't know if you're ready or even looking but I just gave your name to a church in Georgia."

While I had several opportunities and inquiries, my wife and I were not actively looking to leave our ministry, workplace, home in the country, and friends of twelve years. We were comfortable and accustomed to our lives in Ohio.

Two days later, I received a phone call from Clarence Cooley, the church administrator at a church in Marietta, Georgia. Yes — the same church Terry Herald had shared my name with.

Following that initial phone call, my wife and I began praying and within a week, we had made arrangements for me to visit the church with an interest in moving to serve with that church. Within six weeks, I was on my way to Georgia to accept a position on staff at that church.

Our comfort level had been upended by God. Not that anything was wrong, but God simply removed our comfort level as an obstacle. I love adventure, and God replaced our current comfort level with a promising adventure — following Him. Human nature dictates that to move from a current comfort level, individuals must realize the reward on the other side of obedience is greater than the risk we are taking by leaving our comfort zone.

About three months prior to my phone call with Terry Herald, I had three or four conversations with people about serving with other churches and denominational roles. I had not been looking for any of these. I turned each of those down. God had not impressed upon me that it was time to make a ministry move.

At the time of each of these conversations I did not realize God was preparing me mentally and spiritually for this upcoming move. My wife, Pam, and I did not go looking for this move or change of life. But we were willing to follow God if this is what He desired.

The church we were currently at was growing, both in number and spiritually. Our Bible study attendance was growing at a rate above ten percent each year. Ministry to one another and to the community was ever-expanding. God was adding to our number each week.

In addition to my ministry at this church, I was leading training conferences within and across the state of Ohio. Not only were we comfortable, God's presence on the ministry in Ohio was apparent. This can make it challenging to identify God's leading to a different ministry.

God revealed to Pam and me His desire and purpose in various ways; through His people in Georgia and Ohio, through prayer, and through Scripture. One thing God taught us is to always be watchful of where God is at work. It was obvious — God was at work and wanted us to move.

It was difficult saying goodbye to so many wonderful friends and neighbors in Ohio. God opened a door and prepared the way. Our obedience was to walk through that door. We did not lose any of those friends. Though we did put some miles between us, we still to this day communicate with many of those and social media keeps us in touch with many others.

In all of our lives, as we follow God in obedience to His Calling and desires, He gives us situations, victories, and memorable occurrences. I call these spiritual markers. Think of markers you see on the road as you travel. These are mile markers, road signs, and special locations that direct you on your journey, keeping you informed that you are on the right path. Reflect on your journey to date, identify and journal God's spiritual markers in your life — it's an encouraging experience.

As I stood, voice quivering, to read my resignation to our church family in Ohio, I shared some of the spiritual markers in our lives and how, in following those spiritual markers and God's Word, Pam and I knew this was God's plan, not man's. Even when it means leaving everything you know that's comfortable and even fruitful, following God's plan and His timing always proves to be the right path and the correct door to walk through.

"Now the LORD said to Abram, 'Go forth from your country, and from your relatives and from your father's house, to the land which I will show you' (Gen. 12:2).

When God Calls you to a new place of service, He will also provide you with the assurance that it is God's plan, not man's.

Jehovah-Jireh, God is my provider!

Best Intentions Are Not Always the Best Path

Two months earlier, I would not have believed you if you said I would be starting a new ministry position two states away. Yet, this is exactly the situation in which I found myself. As in any new position there was excitement and angst about what was to be, how I would be accepted and what God (and others) would expect of me.

Ministry with God is great, but it is not always easy. After all, as a leader in the church you have many people vying to tell you what to do and how to do it. In a church of 150, you're likely to have at least 155 of these. I was welcomed by most of this church, but held at arm's length by others. This was a very traditional church in many ways.

On an earlier get-acquainted visit to the church, I was introduced to the staff, deacons, and other leaders, and received a tour of the nice, well-maintained facilities including a beautiful sanctuary, plenty of usable education space for Bible study classes, a cozy fireside fellowship hall, a bus barn, and a Family Life Center complete with a gym, showers, exercise room, kitchen, and education space. There was one thing I noticed on this tour, though, that seemed out of place to me: the chairs.

The chairs in the education rooms were older office chairs. Having worked with churches for some time, I understood exactly how these chairs had been acquired. For decades, most churches purchased what they could afford, usually metal folding chairs or hard plastic stackable chairs. However, some churches have members who watch for something better. And when an opportunity is found, especially when something is free, the church becomes the recipient of discarded furniture and other goods.

Church leaders confirmed my assumption. These chairs were donated to the church by a couple different businesses as those businesses updated their office furniture. While the businesses were ready to discard these chairs for newer, updated ones, they were still good chairs when the church received them. However, looking at the colors and styles of the chairs that day, it was obvious these were donated to the church three to four decades earlier.

Opening the door to one classroom, I counted thirty-one chairs. Of those thirty-one, there were nineteen different styles and colors: burnt orange, avocado green, at least three different browns, and styles produced about the time Elvis was a rising star. As stated earlier, this is not the first church where I had seen such outdated furniture — "but it was free."

I prayed about it and settled in my heart on what to do. One of my first week's in the church, I made reference to the hodge-podge of outdated chairs and committed to give $500 towards the first shipment of new, more comfortable chairs. There was no negative feedback. After all, it was quite hard to argue with the datedness of the chairs or someone's donation of $500.

I ordered a sample chair — nice, new chrome-framed with a four-inch cushioned seat. The day the sample chair came in, there were four or five senior adult ladies working in the kitchen. I asked their opinion and had them sit in it (one at a time of course). They all gave positive remarks. No one complained.

We ordered the chairs and several weeks later, on the day the chairs were delivered, I received a call from our church administrator.

"Where do you want them to go?" he asked. "What classes get the first ones?"

A good question. There was no quandary in my mind.

"Seniors. Start with the largest senior adult class," I stated. So that's where we put them. That Sunday and for some time afterwards, those chairs caused the biggest ruckus. You would have thought that I had brought in five-gallon buckets for our seniors to sit on.

It was almost a year before I realized the actual issue. We had bought more of the chairs for other classrooms by this time and they were welcomed by the other classes. On one occasion, I went into the class that received the first chairs to share my appreciation of the years of service to the church. I was not met with open arms.

One ninety-two-year-old lady in the back of the room (in one of the old chairs they had rescued) stood and said, "George, you have done nothing since you got here but try to rip this church apart."

Where did that come from? I wondered. Wounded in spirit, I attempted to handle her comment very politely before exiting the classroom.

After that near-homicidal mission, I was speaking with a couple ladies from that classroom. They weren't exactly apologetic for the scene from that previous Sunday, but one said, "George, those chairs you bought us, we can't get out of them. They don't have arms. We need the chair arms to get out of chairs."

That, my friends, was the reason for the almost year's worth of backlash. I was about forty and they were in their late sixties and seventies. I didn't have issues getting out of chairs. But they did.

I had not considered their need for chair arms. It never occurred to me. We could have spent an extra five dollars per chair and appeased this need for our senior adults and possibly avoided the anguish of these dear senior saints. I never bothered to ask and until that conversation, no one in the class had considered informing me or anyone else of the issue.

My intentions were noble and I had the best possible intentions. It is hard to attract and keep new people in a church when a portion of your facility or furniture is decades outdated. I wanted to encourage the church to bring this part of its furnishings up-to-date. While I had some of the ladies from that class sit in the sample chair, I failed to ask them to point out any issues their contemporaries might have with the chairs.

God taught me a valuable lesson about observation and intentions through that experience. Matthew 14 records a story of Jesus teaching a similar lesson to His disciples.

He'd been teaching all day to a large crowd. "As evening approached, the disciples came to him and said, 'This is a remote place, and it's already getting late. Send the crowds away, so they can go to the villages and buy themselves some food.' Jesus replied, 'They do not need to go away. You give them something to eat.' 'We have here only five loaves of bread and two fish,' they answered" (Matt. 14:15–17).

The disciples had good intentions: "Send them away so they can go eat" (v. 15).

Good intentions, yes.

But Jesus had an even greater lesson to teach. He took the five loaves and two fish and fed the entire crowd of more than 5,000 people.

Observe and don't jump ahead of God with your good intentions. Jehovah-Jireh, God is my provider.

That ninety-two-year-young lady, the day I announced my resignation, now about ninety-four, came to me, took both my hands in hers and said, "George, we did not always see eye to eye (a gross understatement), but you are a good man."

As the saying goes, all's well that ends well, right?

A Long-Term Headache

Six months after our wedding day, Pam suffered an excruciating, alarming headache. It would last for a little more than a month solid, without relief. The headache was so severe that I could not get close to Pam's right temporal lobe, not even with a pointing finger. To get within two inches of that spot would cause her to scream with pain as if she was being hit with a sledgehammer.

Naturally, I carried her to the hospital within a few hours of its onset. Pam was admitted and remained in the hospital for seven days heavily medicated in a darkened room.

After a few days, I realized there was no real process for healing being offered. While X-rays, spinal taps, and other tests were run, no resolutions or remedies were offered.

Pam spent those seven days so drugged up she could not even speak in full sentences — mostly because of the medicine, but also due to the pain. On the seventh day, I checked her out of the hospital and took her home for the night.

Within twenty-four hours we had admitted her to another hospital. At this hospital, we worked with a neurologist who specializes in severe headaches.

On the day Pam was admitted, he was in Michigan completing final paperwork for the research and testing of a new procedure for this very type of headache that he and a Michigan doctor had developed. He was made aware of Pam's condition and flew back to Ohio to oversee Pam's care. There were also at least two other patients who would be in this first round of treatments.

The next couple of days were filled with more tests, exams, and bloodwork. This time was also used to clean Pam's system of any lingering narcotics from the first hospital visit and to adjust her diet for the coming procedure. Then the actual procedure would begin.

The actual treatment would take six days with one injection each day. The medication was extremely powerful and could only be implemented in a specific sequence. The first day, she would be given a small, closely monitored dose. The amount would be increased a little each of the second and third days in precise increments. Then the fourth, fifth, and sixth days, it would be decreased in the same precise increments. Testing had shown the human body could not take this medication in any other fashion.

Pam began experiencing relief on the fourth and fifth day. On the seventh day, the headache was gone. The procedure had worked! She was nearly pain free, but she remained in the hospital for a few more days under observation for side effects, withdrawals, or complications. They also used this period to find the right prescription of medication to keep the headaches from returning.

The human body has a particular gland that produces a certain secretion helpful to our brain function in that part of the head. It was discovered that Pam's gland was producing up to one hundred times above the normal amount. This overabundance was causing the inflammation and neurologic infirmity. Finding this out was actually good news as our concerns had turned to the possibility of brain cancer or other permanent, debilitating conditions. I feared losing my wife of only six months. It was a very harrowing time.

Life changed for us in some ways. We would not have children due to the strong medications that Pam would be on — potentially for the rest of her life. Her diet had to be altered, which meant we altered mine as well.

Some life changes were small, some were not so small. Our bond to one another and our longing to not be away from each other also strengthened greatly.

Through the next ten years, Pam was monitored and observed by this neurologist and his team of doctors. Her medications were changed a couple of times due the adverse effects they can have on the body, but the prognosis was that she would never come off some type of drugs to help her maintain her health.

Ten years later, we were leading a group of five couples through a very in-depth, comprehensive Bible study titled Experiencing God. Unbeknownst to anyone in the group, including me, Pam asked God to heal her and to take away her need for the medications. She began cutting back, which she had tried twice before without success. Trying to wean herself had both times brought on setbacks and the headache returned.

This time however, she had no ill effects, no setbacks, and no headaches. This time, she had asked God to remove the disorder and to heal her, taking away the need for medication. As I write this more than twenty years later, Pam has not had a severe headache, nor has she ever had to take medicine for the malady in her temporal lobe since God's healing.

God is a great God. We do not know why she had this happen or why she had to suffer the month-long severe headache or the ten years of medication and restrictions. But we do not question why. We praise God for His undeniable healing of her body. The ten-year mark proved to be God's perfect timing. Three months after healing Pam's body, God moved us to another state to serve him. A move that took us away from the doctor who had treated Pam and watched over her health for ten years.

We know there was more than a doctor watching over Pam all those years. And He, God, healed her just before He would move us to our next chapter on the journey of life.

Luke 9:37-43 tells the story of a boy prone to seizures, possessed by a demon. The disciples could not heal the boy or cast out the demon. Yet, Jesus had no difficulty. The boy was healed instantly and handed back to his father.

God is the great physician, and, in His timing, He can heal all diseases. Verse 43 says all the people around were amazed. Pam and I too were amazed, and I stand in awe today at God's healing work in her life.

Jehovah-Jireh, God will provide!

Father's Day Reflection

It was May 1988. I was living in Ohio and traveled home to Kentucky to visit my mom, dad and fiancé, Pam, every time I could get a couple days off. On this particular trip, I purchased something I first saw on a lakeshore in Ohio — stunt kites. My purchase was a set of three Tilby stunt kites — a Tilby Trilogy. Each kite in this set carried the traditional diamond shape.

With a normal kite you attach a ball of string, launch the kite and let it climb into the air while you hold the ball of string releasing it little by little allowing the kite to climb higher. A traditional kite will dance and wave in the air a little, but not much.

A stunt kite on the other hand will do much more. It has two lines attached to the front of the first kite. One line attaches on the cross rib, just left of center. The other just right of center. In this case, I had purchased a trilogy or three kites you would fly stacked together attached by three lines. Three kites in a row, one in front of the other about 2 feet apart. Each kite was a different color (red, yellow, orange), each with a striped pattern and each had a fifty-foot tail of the main color of the kite to which it was attached.

Using the two strings you could get the kite in the air and do tricks and spins, dives and climbs. Whereas a traditional kite stays stationary, a stunt kite will fly across the skies. By pulling on the left cord you can drive the kite to the left, then quickly spin it to drive the opposite direction. Starting at seventy-five feet in the air you can pull one cord and cause the kite(s) to dive straight towards the ground or dive in a series of tight circles. Then reversing your hand position, have it climb back in a similar circular fashion.

I had fun with those kites over the years as they moved with us to Georgia and on to California before I sold them to another would-be enthusiast. But, by far, my greatest memory with those kites was the day I bought them.

I sat on the living room floor of my parents' house and put them together. Though I did not do it alone. My father, a heart patient, got down on the floor with me, just like when I was a child. Helping one another, laughing and talking as we worked. It was a joint venture. Me at thirty-one years of age and Dad at fifty-seven, I truly believe he was as enthused as I was.

Of course, as soon as they were assembled, I wanted to try them out. I asked my father to go with me, but he was too tired and worn out. Putting those kites together was the last thing my father and I would do together. He passed away to his eternal glory two weeks later. As I write this, it has been thirty-one years since his passing. I was thirty-one years old, and yet, I have never forgotten the look on his face and the joy of putting those kites together on the floor; just a father and his son.

Reflecting on this, I'm reminded of many Scriptures where God describes Himself as Father. I ponder the thoughts that if my earthly father and I could enjoy such wonderful experiences and capture them as wonderful memories, how much more my Heavenly Father, God Himself, relishes in the experiences I share with Him in His divine plan.

In Jeremiah 29:11, God reveals the following truth for us: "For I know the plans I have for you" — this is the LORD's declaration — "Plans for your well-being, not for disaster, to give you a future and a hope. Then you will call upon Me and come and pray to Me, and I will hear you. You will seek Me and find Me, when you seek Me with all your heart."

I know my earthly father always wanted the best for me and each of my siblings. I also know the pleasure it brought to him when each of us spent quality time with him.

Building kites may be fun, but it was also quality time with my father. Memories that I cherish to this day. God has blessed me, providing me with memories like this one. Each of our lives is filled with God's blessings and memories. These are some of my thoughts as we recently celebrated another Father's Day. Cherish the times. Cherish the memories. Cherish life.

Dad, like the Apostle Paul, I can say, "I give thanks to my God for every remembrance of you" (Phil. 1:3).

Jehovah-Jireh, God is my provider!

God's Plans are Greater, and His Timing is Perfect

While serving on staff at a church in Marietta, Georgia, I was at our association office, utilizing some of their resources. In the denomination I serve, associations are not hierarchical. Every church is autonomous and self-governing. The upper judicatories exist to assist and resource the local church.

David Suddath, one of the associational leaders, walked into the room and asked, "Hey George, do you want to go to California on a missions trip?"

I threw my hand up as if to vote, and replied, "Count me in."

"Good," came David's reply. "You go home and write what we're going to do and we'll go."

Now, to be fair, there was a little interaction between my "count me in," and David's "write it up" response. Three of us made plans and traveled to California's central coast region to consult with churches for a week. We were able to visit and consult with fourteen different churches — all experiencing a plateau or decline.

It was a really good week and we were able to see some sights and visit parts of the country we had never before seen. I paid my own way out there — my contribution to California.

It was a one-week trip, and that, in my mind, was to be my only interaction with the state of California. However, while on that trip, God burdened my heart for the lack of leadership development in churches of that region. The west coast is a long way off from the stronger, larger concentration of churches and equipping events available in the southeast and Midwest.

Our mission trip to California was in March. Fast-forward to the end of July. I had been praying for the churches in the central coast region, as God had not let me forget the burden He had laid on my heart.

After speaking with my pastor, I made a phone call to the associational leader whom we had worked with on that trip, Dr. Mike Stewart.

Dr. Stewart is the associational missionary for churches from, at that time, San Mateo to King City, California. That stretches from just south of San Francisco, through all of Silicon Valley, to the southern end of the Salinas Valley. 80% of the nations' bagged salads, lettuce, etc. comes from the Salinas Valley. So the churches in this region must reach the multimillion-dollar techies of Silicon Valley and the thousands of migrant workers in the fields of Salinas Valley and every cultural landing in between.

My reason for calling Dr. Stewart was to offer one week each month (or every other month) to come to California to work with his churches and pastors in building leaders and discipleship processes. At the end of the call, Dr. Stewart asked to pray about my proposal and to take it to his administration council.

Two weeks later, Dr. Stewart made the follow-up phone call to me. After our greetings to each other, Dr. Stewart brought up my proposal and said, "We don't think that is what God wants. We believe God wants you out here full time."

To which I quickly responded, "Thanks, but no thanks. I know God is leading me in that ministry direction (building leaders in multiple churches), but not in California."

I had had seven similar opportunities in other states and never believed it to be God's timing. Now, however, God would not let me rest.

It was easy to tell Mike Stewart no. God, on the other hand, doesn't always take no for an answer. A reading of the story of Jonah will demonstrate the effects on your life when you say no to God.

Seven months after my phone call to Dr. Stewart, Pam and I were living in California, where I would work with Mike Stewart and the Central Coast Baptist Association of churches for nearly seven years before God would move us on to our next chapter in ministry. It was a great seven years.

My wife, Pam, and I would never have dreamed of living in California. We had never even entertained the idea of a vacation in California. But now, we were living there, in a beautiful region of God's great creation.

We lived in Gilroy, a smaller city thirty miles south of San Jose and Silicon Valley. Gilroy is known as "The Garlic Capital of the World." While they no longer grow the majority of the world's garlic, they do package and produce the largest percentage of the world's garlic. At one time Gilroy also had a tomato packing plant.

It is said that when the tomato packing plant and the garlic plant were both operating at the same time, the aroma was so good that you could cook pasta, sit outside, and enjoy the pasta without any sauce.

In addition to the garlic and beautiful scenery, Gilroy is also said to be only one of four places in the world with a Mediterranean climate — and we enjoyed it all seven years of our residence there.

The ministry flourished. God blessed our ministry and many of the churches we served. We were able to provide unparalleled training in that region, for many ministry areas.

God's plans are greater than your plans or my plans. While Pam and I never thought of moving to California, God had plans for us to not only live and work there, but to also pour into the lives of others as God poured into us through others in our time there.

As an added bonus, God gave us the enjoyment of the vast array of His creation. So much to see, so much variety, so much beauty. And we found the people in California to be as beautiful as the scenery and as gracious as the south. Jehovah-Jireh, God is my provider!

God's plans are greater and His timing is perfect. As Proverbs 16:9 states, "The heart of man plans his way, but the Lord establishes his steps."

Treat the Cause, Not the Symptom

While living in Georgia, Pam, my wife, developed a severe back pain issue. We had no idea what brought this ailment about. She had no accidents or any instance that we could point to for causing this injury. She was accustomed to chiropractic treatments, so she continued going to the offices of two young Christian chiropractors. Within a few short months they had her back to good health.

A year afterwards came God's calling for us to serve in California. Pam had at least three good years before the back pain returned. Looking back, we see God's hand in using those two young Christian chiropractors to re-establish Pam's health so we could move to California in service to Him.

After a couple of years in California, the pain returned. My wife suffered from chronic back pain for several years. The pain and debilitation became severe and was interrupting her life, health, and well-being. For two years, we drove the sixty-mile round trip to see her doctor every four to six weeks.

It was during this time that I realized why a Health Maintenance Organization (HMO) actually exists. The doctors kept telling Pam that they were trying to help her manage the pain. To this she replied, "I do not want to manage the pain; I want to get rid of the pain."

The doctors tried different types of therapy and management techniques for several months to no avail. Afterwards, they began giving Pam injections of different medications.

Every four to six weeks, Pam received another injection, something different from the last. The epidurals and blocks were just masks for the pain, not a potential healer. The injections were mere attempts to mask the pain, to keep Pam from feeling the pain. Each injection attempted to temporarily mask and hide the pain. One thing I feared with these injections was that Pam could easily cause more damage to her back without knowing - for the few injections that actually did hide the pain.

When I asked the doctor why they were only treating symptoms and not trying to treat the cause of the pain or correct the damage, his reply to me was, "That's not what we do here. We help you manage the pain."

This was one of the largest HMO's in the nation, the largest on the west coast. Our conversation carried on for a couple more minutes, though nothing changed — nothing except our resolve.

Pam and I avoided her having traditional back surgery because of the people we had known in our lives who had multiple back surgeries, often without much, if any, improvement. But a time came when Pam said, "I can't take this any longer. I've got to have relief. I'll have the surgery."

When she revealed this to her doctor, he said they would not conduct surgery on her because her back was not "bad enough." Pam had four herniated, or bulging, discs. This doctor had seen her deteriorating condition yet wanted to keep treating her with blocks. We asked for a second opinion. Staying within the same HMO we found another specialist in Oakland, California.

On the first visit, this doctor reviewed Pam's charts and images. His opinion: "We won't do surgery on you because you have too much damage."

Two doctors from the same HMO gave completely opposite diagnoses. Pam was on the prayer lists of family, our church, and many others across the nation. We updated our prayer needs that day.

A friend called us and asked to come over that evening. This was not uncommon as we often spent time in each others' homes.

Sitting in our living room that evening, John said, "I had what you have, ten years ago. I had two bulging discs and had surgery in India" — his home country. He went on to say, "I have not had back pain or issues since."

Pam and John both got on the internct later and one of them located a back surgeon in the Bay Area, about two hours away from our home, who performed this type of surgery. This too was a miracle of God.

At that time, he was perhaps the only physician in the U.S. performing this type of surgery and we lived less than two hours from him. This was a physician with training in the U.S. and years of performing traditional back surgeries.

He changed his technique a few years earlier when he developed similar back issues of his own and knew that what he did for a living was not the answer. He went out of the country to have this surgery. Completely healed, he learned how to perform this surgery himself and the remainder of his career only performed this one type of back surgery.

My wife had the surgery — she had four bulging and herniated discs. It was done as two outpatient surgeries. One where two of the discs were taken care of on Tuesday, and the other two on Thursday. There was no incision, only four tiny puncture marks. All four discs were repaired.

My wife has not had one minute of back pain since the surgery in April of 2006. She was cured — completely healed. We paid several deca-thousand dollars out of pocket for my wife to have the surgery, but it was the best investment we ever made. Thank you to John and Sam for your revelation of the surgical procedure and your investment in Pam's healing!

I share this story with you because our personal life and church life often become much like the first set of doctors treating Pam's health issues with her back. We look for symptoms and think we can "fix" the problem by addressing the symptom. Oftentimes, like the doctors, all we are doing is hiding the pain. The issue of decline is still with us. A drop in attendance is a symptom, not a cause.

Example: A church that realizes it has wandered away from reaching out to the community may react by offering more classes on evangelism and addressing the need to reach out through other means, messages, and slogans. While these may be helpful, without providing the church members opportunities and practical applications to practice their ability and faith, little will change. The emphasis becomes more classes, not more outreach opportunities.

In the church today, and in much of our life, we spend the majority of our time treating symptoms, not causes. We are trying only to hide the pain.

Begin right now praying and thinking through the difference of symptoms and causes for your current situation in life and those of your church or organization.

We praise God daily for Pam's healing.

Jehovah-Jireh, God is my provider!

Listening for God's Directive

God's calling on our lives is to follow Him. It is to serve Him where He leads us. I have found following God's calling on my life to be very fulfilling, satisfying, and rewarding. But the reward is not financial wealth — that is not God's intent. He does, however, meet and exceed all our needs. In my opinion, the rewards of following God's calling far surpass financial gain.

One thing that I've learned, and caution others on, is that God will not act in the same manner every time He has a directive or change for you. In other words, you cannot expect God's plan to unfold in steps one, two, three, and four the same as the last time He called you to change your serving directive, led you to a new area of ministry, or moved you. God's ultimate directive for His believers is to fulfill the Great Commission. His personal directives call for us to move in obedience to Him in fulfilling that overarching directive — to make His Kingdom known.

As you read this book, you will read of at least four times when God changed our directive. Each time was different, and I love it, because you have to have faith in God to follow obediently. Each time God called us to change our directive, He used different means. Each time, we learned more about God and true faith, and with each change we grew spiritually.

For every one of His believers and followers, each time we act in obedience to God, a great reward is ours on the other side of obedience. This does not mean we will never face hardship and distraction — we will. Yet, God's rewards far outweigh the difficulties we face.

As we prepared for our move to California from Georgia, we promised God we would not close the door until we knew He had closed that door. As mentioned in an earlier part of this book, we were not looking to move to California. This was not even remotely on our radar of places to live and serve. We had never even considered a vacation in California. We do, however, try to live by faith and follow God's directive.

Before our move, on a visit to California, we carried with us a list Pam had drawn up. It was a list of our current expenses in Georgia, our monthly bills, our insurance rates, even a grocery receipt, so we could compare prices of groceries where we currently lived in Georgia to where we would be in California, if God so moved. This grocery comparison alone might have been enough to stop some people from making the move. Every item we looked at cost at least double in California. If we paid fifty-eight cents for a can of corn in Georgia, the same brand in California was $1.20. Every single item on our list was at least double. Not only groceries, but also utilities, insurance, gasoline, and don't forget, rent. Everything costs more in California — a lot more.

After our visit, we kept our promise to God. We could have said there's no way. We cannot do it. Pam and I could have said that God is closing the door. But, we did not.

We continued talking with those in California who we would be working with. Everything looked good to go — with one exception. The highest remuneration they could squeeze out of their budget was going to be $10,000 short of what we needed to live in that part of California. That would certainly be a door closer, right?

For some, yes. In other situations, perhaps. However, because of what we had witnessed God do in our lives in past transitions, the spiritual markers erected, we knew this was not a door closer. It was indeed going to require an act of faith. It required that we trust God with everything.

We were moving all the way across the country from one coast to the other. If it did not work out, if we read God wrong, we were toast. We would be so broke that we likely would not be able to afford to move back. In faith, we made the arrangements and began preparing for the move to follow in obedience to God's directive though the financial provision was $10,000 short.

You've heard the expression, "Nothing is impossible for God." Well, certainly this transition in ministry was not. Not only did God make it possible, it was seven years of remarkable experiences: the beautiful scenery with multiple landscapes of God's differing creation, the Mediterranean climate, the wonderful people we were blessed to work with and serve across the region and the state. But on top of all of these is the spiritual growth it provided in preparation for what God has had me doing since He changed our directive and called us to leave California.

As for that $10,000 shortage? We never missed a meal or a bill. In fact, we even paid Pam's back surgery bills of over $35,000 out-of-pocket and never missed a beat. We did not make payments, we did not take out a loan. We paid cash for her surgery. God did inspire one other couple who gave us $5,000 for her surgery. To whom we are very grateful. When God's directives lead you somewhere you believe you cannot go — don't run away from them. Run as fast as you can, headfirst into them. You will be blessed beyond measure!

"And he said, "Go out and stand on the mount before the LORD." And behold, the LORD passed by, and a great and strong wind tore the mountains and broke in pieces the rocks before the LORD, but the LORD was not in the wind. And after the wind an earthquake, but the LORD was not in the earthquake. ¹² And after the earthquake a fire, but the LORD was not in the fire. And after the fire the sound of a low whisper. ¹³ And when Elijah heard it, he wrapped his face in his cloak and went out and stood at the entrance of the cave. And behold, there came a voice to him and said, "What are you doing here, Elijah?" (1 Kings 9:11-13)

Sometimes we look for God only in the big, extraordinary things, yet He often speaks to us through the smallest whisper. For Elijah, it was not strong wind, earthquake, or fire. It was a low whisper.

For us, on this occasion, it was an open door that seemed unlikely and against all human reasoning. There were plenty of opportunities for Pam and me to say, "Nope. This looks like a door closer to us," but because of the spiritual markers in our life, we realized it was one more step of deeper faith in our Lord, God Almighty.

Listening for God's directives means abandoning self-interests and being still before God.

Jehovah-Jireh, God is my provider!

Blessed Through Prayer

I have been in New Testament evangelical churches all my life. Well, except for that five- or six-year period in my late teens and early twenties. Perhaps we'll cover those in another book.

In church, we are taught certain disciplines – spiritual disciplines. The greatest of these is prayer. We are taught to pray certain prayers found in the Bible and other prayers at mealtime and bedtime. As we grow and mature spiritually, we are taught how to pray.

Prayer is simply a two-way conversation with God. However, most of our prayers are more monologue than dialogue. We do all the talking and expect God to do all the listening. Then we expect Him to act on our prayers and petitions exactly as we desire and, in our timing — which is usually right now.

Newsflash — God does not work that way. Eventually, with proper maturing, we learn that prayer is not about getting God to go along with our desires, but to align our hearts with God's plan and timing.

There are many great prayers in the Bible. Prayers that we can and should pray to intersect our lives today.

One such prayer is found in the Old Testament book of 1 Chronicles. It is known as the prayer of Jabez. One thing I have learned is that if something is recorded in the Bible, it is not there for a history lesson, it is not there for filler. It is in God's Holy Scripture because there is a lesson that I need to learn to help me in my life.

The first nine chapters of 1 Chronicles is a genealogy of the nation of Israel, beginning with Adam and going through to their return from captivity in the sixth century BC. And right in the middle of all those genealogic verses are these two verses. They appear somewhat out of place with the surrounding chapters. God stops the roll call of the Hebrew nation to tell us of this man, Jabez, and his prayer.

I often pray Jabez's prayer found in 1 Chronicles 4:10: "And Jabez called on the God of Israel saying, 'Oh, that You would bless me indeed, and enlarge my territory, that Your hand would be with me, and that You would keep me from evil, that I may not cause pain!' So God granted him what he requested."

It is short, but it is a true blessing to be able to pray it and watch God move in my life. Yet, it is not reserved for me or a select few. It is in the

Holy Scriptures because God wants to bless the life of everyone who will earnestly pray as Jabez prayed — with a sincere heart and a willingness to follow God no matter how different it looks from what you desire. Notice, Jabez did not ask for specifics. Whatever God chose to give him was indeed a blessing.

The key to being blessed by God through this prayer is praying in earnest and with a sincere heart, not expecting specifics from God. Most of our prayers are not in earnest — even in our worship services. The majority of our prayer lives consist of rote and ritualistic prayers. We have learned well to pray from our head — praying what we've heard others pray and what sounds good.

God's desire, though, is that we pray from our heart. He does not want us to quote someone else's prayer. He desires us to pour out our heart with a yearning to accept His will for our life.

Oh, to be able to relate to you how God has blessed me through prayers from the heart without strings attached. But then I would need to tell you of the times I failed God and others in futile prayer or no prayer at all.

While prayer has been a part of my life for years, as I've grown older, I have truly studied Scripture, books about prayer, discipleship courses on prayer and people praying. And in recent years, I have studied prayer with a partner — the perfect prayer partner: God! With God as my prayer partner, I am truly blessed!

As I have prayed the prayer of Jabez (with a few changes) over the past ten to twelve years, it is usually asking God to give me more opportunities to serve Him. I stay busy as a church health strategist, assisting churches and denominational entities, and public speaking engagements. Well, as busy as I want.

Yet, I often find myself praying the Jabez prayer because I crave being blessed by God. Once you experience the blessing on the other side of obedience to God, you want more. And therein lies the key to blessings. It is obedience to God's call on your life — both your life's calling and what He desires for you on any particular day.

I cannot tell you how many times I have prayed Jabez's prayer for God to bless me and enlarge my territory, and within the hour (sometimes as I say, "Amen") my phone will ring or an email will appear in my inbox with an opportunity to serve God. It might be an invitation for a speaking engagement, or it might be a troubled pastor, needing to vent or someone to pray with.

It could be easy to think, "Yeah, George, you're asking for more work for more money." But, if those are your thoughts, you clearly do not know me. I do not charge for ministry speaking engagements. My remuneration comes through honorariums and love gifts. But I never charge for ministry engagements. And there is never any remuneration for phone calls, texts, emails, advice, or prayer. The blessings that I receive are greater than money.

Here's a sample of how I pray Jabez's prayer: "Lord, You have blessed me indeed. My blessing is in being able to serve You. Oh, that You would bless me indeed, and enlarge my territory in whatever way you desire. And Lord keep Your hand upon me, that You would keep me from evil, that I may not bring shame on You, Your church or my family! In Jesus' precious name. Amen!"

Lessons learned: Prayer is essential in my life. The more I can align my prayer life to God's desires for me, the more blessings will be poured out allowing me to serve Him more.

Jehovah-Jireh, God is indeed my provider!

Life's Lessons From God thru Bob

Bob is a devoted husband, father, hard worker, and member of a church I served. He attended church services every week, sitting with his wife, and was a great handyman who worked in construction. Bob and his wife are wonderful people. I am honored to call them friends. They enjoy having people in their home. I cherish the times Pam and I were invited into their home for a meal and conversation.

The one thing I just didn't get about Bob was why he did not regularly attend Sunday School. Was there something missing in Bob's Christianity? I mean, certainly, according to the standards of mainline denominations, you could not be a real committed Christian unless you were actively involved in Sunday School, right?

Now, I am a Sunday School/small group Bible study guy. I truly believe in it and that everyone should be involved and engaged in the Christian life through small group Bible study. Yet, this is how God used Bob and taught me a valuable lesson that churches need to understand and learn in this twenty-first century in which we live.

It is my recollection that Bob had been actively involved in Sunday School as an adult. However, the teacher of Bob's class, the kind of teacher you want to clone for all your adult classes, moved across the country with his job and Bob's wife stepped out of the class to teach in the children's area. The class was in decline.

At one point, Bob began a larger remodel project at our church. He was there every day after working his normal construction job. He would arrive about 3:30 or 4:00 p.m. each day and stay until long after I was gone for the day.

A couple of times each week, I made it a point to go to the area of the church where Bob was working and spend some time with him. Bob and I were friends, but I wanted him to know I appreciated him for using his gifts and to offer help if I could. I also thought I might get to talk with him about Sunday School and perhaps at least learn of his reasons for what I considered scattered attendance.

In my visits with Bob at the church worksite, God began to reveal to me a lesson He wanted me to learn through Bob. In my casual conversations with Bob, I learned that Bob stopped at the same restaurant every weekday morning oftentimes carrying his Bible in and studying while eating. This drew attention to himself and gave him opportunities to pray for the staff, customers, and others. It also gave Bob opportunities for spiritual conversations. I also learned of other things Bob was doing outside the church demonstrating his Christianity.

Always serving others with his skills and abilities, if he heard of someone in need of some home repairs, Bob was there. And he never charged. At one point, Pam and I wanted to do some remodeling of a large room in our home. Bob heard about it and came to the rescue. He and another gentleman from the church, Doug, completed the entire job: the tear out, which is major in itself, and the complete remodel. And he would not accept a dime in payment. He even furnished some of the materials and would not accept reimbursement.

He did relent saying, "If you want to do anything, make a contribution to the youth ministry of the church." If he wasn't going to accept any payment, we would do as he suggested. Especially since Doug, his coworker, also did not accept anything and was a key leader in the youth ministry.

The first lesson God taught me through Bob was that he was probably getting more Bible study than ninety percent of the people attending Bible study classes.

The second lesson was that Bob was actually putting his Christianity into practice every day.

Bob was doing for others, using his gifts and talents and serving those who had needs. This is what we want taught in Sunday School, yet, it is rarely practiced in such a manner by attendees. Few members of any church I've known served as Bob did.

The main lesson God taught me through Bob was that it's not always about attending what I want people to attend. It is about truly serving God — which is what we teach in every Bible study class and every sermon. God's question to me, "Which is more important, people in class or people out demonstrating the love of Christ through obedience and service?" The answer is simple and straightforward. The Christian life is about serving.

God was teaching Bob through his daily Bible study at breakfast and at night in his home, in weekly worship services, and in his relationships. He was also around other men, Doug, myself and other church members, living out the Bible. Iron sharpening iron.

I've watched Bob, on church workdays, engage men younger in the faith with biblical practices and conversations. Bob is a true practicing disciple of Christ willing to engage others in plain, simple language while using his gifts, strengths, and talents.

The people Christ often recognized as true men and women of faith were not the ones who could check off the religious boxes. Those Christ recognized were those like the centurion (Luke 8:5-13) and the woman who gave less than all others, but still gave all she had (Luke 21:1-4).

Jesus tells us in Scripture that you are likely to hear one of two responses from God: "Well done, good and faithful servant" or "Depart from me, you wicked and lazy person."

Contrary to mainline religious thinking of our day, Christ does not say "Well done, thou good and faithful attender." Being an active attendee in the body of Christ is important for you and others in the body of Christ. Yet, God used Bob to teach me valuable lessons about serving.

I am still a small group Bible study man, but I am so grateful God put Bob in my life to teach me valuable lessons. As we look to grow disciples, let us also rethink what it means to be a disciple and how to lead in new directions of Christianity — everyone using his or her gifts and talents to serve outside the church building. Putting Christianity into practice: this is God's call on our lives. This is maturing disciples.

God is a provider of great lessons.

Jehovah-Jireh, God is my provider!

God's Questions Are Often Rhetorical

"Don't you know I can keep the California connection open no matter where you live?" That is the question posed to me on a cold December day in 2008 as I was driving alone in my car while visiting family over the Christmas break.

Did you catch the fact that I was alone in my car when this question was posed to me? And no, I was not on my cell phone. Though not audibly, the question was clearly addressed to me and was, in my head and heart, as clear as audible. I knew the question was from God Almighty. Yes, He still speaks.

But why this question, on this day? My thoughts were not on moving, not on any California connection, not on ministry at all that particular morning.

I'm actually not certain what my thoughts were on at the time. I just know that question interrupted me out of nowhere. That is another reason I knew it was from God. While my thought patterns that morning were not about moving from California, or any ministry aspect, in recent weeks, I had some random thoughts — out of the blue — of why I could not leave California.

Random thoughts that included:

God was blessing our ministry in California. A growing, flourishing, blessed ministry. We had great friends, beautiful scenery and a nice home we had invested a lot of equity in, in one of only four places on the planet with a Mediterranean climate. Why would I consider leaving?

Why, how, could anyone being blessed by God in so many ways want to leave such a setting? Like I stated earlier, I was not looking to leave. I was very content and blessed. Now, looking back, perhaps those earlier thoughts were God preparing me for the question He would pose in my car that December morning.

In sharing this testimony, I sometimes interpret the God question that morning as, "Are you ready for your next step of faith?"

I let my audience know that was not the actual question God asked that morning, but it was, in reality, what was being asked of me. And, when a question like that comes from God, it is a rhetorical question. One that does not need a response. God is not waiting for you to debate it with Him. In essence He is saying, "Are you ready? Because it is coming."

The actual question, "Don't you know I can keep the California connection open no matter where you live?" is also a rhetorical question. A rhetorical question in which God was not only asking me, but letting me know I was ready, even if I did not realize I was ready.

You see, God does not pose a question like this until He knows you are ready to be used and stretched by Him in a new way. I count myself blessed that God would pose such a question to me.

It was God who prepared me. He brought me through all the experiences, trials, blessings, settings, and situations, preparing me for such a time as this. In addition, the places He had me serve over the years, both in the corporate world and in ministry, and the great spiritual leaders He gave me to work with prepared me all along for this next step of faith.

I called my wife before I got out of the car that morning. We both knew what God was about to do. Well, not exactly, but we knew there was a change coming. Neither of us had any doubts that this was God, and we would be following Him and moving in ministry. And since the question was posed as it was, we understood it also meant we'd likely be making a physical move as well.

We would be leaving our home, our friends and the flourishing ministry in California. Of course, the most difficult part of these moves is always leaving the people you have come to know and love. The logistics of the move would come over the next couple of months, but the calling from God was absolute.

This also meant we would be leaving a regular paying ministry position with benefits and a steady income. Accepting God's next step of ministry for my life meant stepping out a little further in faith, trusting Him to provide for every need in a much more challenging way. God was saying, "There will be no guaranteed check each month from an employer. And what about insurance and other benefits? Do you trust me?"

Truly stepping out like this was raising the bar of our trust in God. We never hesitated, and never looked back. We miss California, the people, the ministry, the blessings. But we have never regretted following the Lord into a new calling — and this last twelve plus years since answering this calling is no different. We are on an amazing ride with God, our Lord and Savior. And it all started with one rhetorical question.

As a young boy, Samuel was living in the temple with the priest Eli. Samuel had not had an experience with God until one particular night when God in an audible voice called out three times to Samuel. Samuel, thinking the voice was Eli calling to him, ran to Eli each time and asked what Eli needed from him. "Then Eli realized that the LORD was calling the boy. ⁹ So Eli told Samuel, "Go and lie down, and if he calls you,

say, 'Speak, LORD, for your servant is listening.'"
So Samuel went and lay down in his place.
The LORD came and stood there, calling as at the
other times, "Samuel! Samuel!" Then Samuel
said, "Speak, for your servant is listening.'" (1
Samuel 3:8–10).

It is good to know the voice of the Lord when He
speaks. As with anyone, to recognize His voice
you must spend time with Him. I can't say I'm
the best at it, but after years of listening,
studying His Word, and paying attention to the
spiritual markers in my life, I am so grateful that
He has allowed me to hear from Him and
willingly respond. I pray that I will be able to do
so in the future.

Oh, by the way, God has allowed me to be back
in California assisting churches and
organizations every year. Let me emphasize that
— every year — since our move away. He truly
has taken care of that "California connection." I
am blessed to serve an amazing, incredible,
rhetorical God.

Jehovah-Jireh, God indeed provides!

Phone Call From A Friend, Hearing From God

Over the years, Mike Perry had become a friend. Mike worked for one of the largest Christian-based organizations in the nation as lead of the Partnership Networks. Mike and I had become acquainted several years prior to the event in this story while I served part time on a contract basis with his organization.

A wise, intelligent, and experienced practitioner, Mike was a mentor to many. Over the years Mike began to ask me to work on some of his projects. I was privileged and honored to work with Mike every chance I could.

I remember long talks in airports waiting on connecting flights or others flying in to join us on some of our ventures. Not to mention the after-hours conversations at conference centers, hotels, and restaurants, and the varied phone calls over the years. Mike not only kept up with my ministry, but he was also an encourager, supporter, and sounding board. But not only to me. I read and heard of Mike speaking to others about our ministry efforts and successes in Georgia, California and afterward.

Before moving from California, I called Mike to let him know what God was leading me to next and that I would be moving to Kentucky. Also in the conversation, I asked Mike if he could consider bringing a team out to work with some of our churches in the transition and after my leaving, so the work of building stronger churches in this California region would continue.

Almost a year after moving to Kentucky, I received a call from Mike Perry. We had not spoken to one another since I left California. Mike is an intelligent and wise man, but he camouflages it well with his likeable personality and his good ol' southern country boy dialect.

"I hear you're pastoring," he said on the phone that day.

"No, just doing an interim pastorate." I shared. An interim pastorate is a short term in between two full-time pastors at a church.

We talked for a few minutes about what was going on in this church, one that had been declining for years. We were starting to see some improvement. No phenomenal growth explosions, but methodical plotting and plodding along. The church had seen a ten percent increase in the few months I was serving with them — and it was the church people doing the legwork along with me.

During that conversation, Mike stated, "If you could write down what you're doing, I talk to pastors every week who need to know it. There are many pastors out there trying to figure that out." Our conversation carried on for a couple more minutes before we said our good-byes.

Following that conversation, God kept bringing that one statement of Mike's back to my mind. "If you could write down what you're doing, I talk to pastors every week who need to know it." I never thought of writing any of it down. I did not even know what "it" was. I was simply following God's lead and doing what I knew to do.

My thoughts then turned to, "What have I seen in the last seventeen years of serving in churches and consulting with and coaching churches that God wanted me to use in my ministry."

I was not looking to write a book, only to find the commonalities of dying churches to avoid and of growing churches to emulate. I wanted to find any similarities that might help churches stave off declining trends and instead turn to healthy growing Great Commission ministries.

About three months later, I was sending the material to my publisher. After much deliberation with several people (publishers and ministers included) a book was born with the title, *Reaching the Summit: Avoiding and Reversing Decline in the Church.* It was God's work, and He was blessing it. Within seven months, the first printing had sold out and we ordered the second printing, doubling the quantity.

This alone was enough to demonstrate that it was God-issued. The book was never in brick and mortar bookstores, and there was never a marketing campaign. The marketing was simply my few speaking engagements and word of mouth. It seemed everyone who read it was sharing it and encouraging others to purchase it as well.

In the years since, a revised version of *Reaching the Summit* has been published with at least two additional printings, and it remains the most sought-after piece I've written, and the highest volume of service I am requested to assist churches with. And it all started with a phone call from a friend and listening to how God was speaking through that phone call.

God speaks in various ways. One of those ways is through other people. God used a man named Ananias to share God's calling with Saul (Acts 9). God used Phillip to assist an Ethiopian Eunuch in understanding God's will for his life (Acts 8).

Throughout Scripture, we read of God using one person to help others find their purpose or calling. Note, Mike was not telling me to write a book. He was inquiring into how my ministry was going. God used Mike that day as part of my continual preparation for my ministry Calling.

Actually, it was in God's plans long before. It is what He knew was to be when He put in my heart to follow Him on a journey that He would reveal as I continued in obedience. The unfolding has been far more and different than I expected. I am extremely blessed to have encouraging friends who check in, friends whom God uses to speak into my life. I am also glad that I've chosen to follow God on His amazing journey for me.

Jehovah-Jireh, God is a wonderful provider!

God's Sweet Spot May Seem Crazy to the World

Earlier in this book, you read of my transitions in ministry settings. The last one being from a position in denominational work in California to full-time service without financial backing.

It is not that I do not get paid, I do. God is gracious. God's calling on my life currently has me serving without any guarantee of pay. There are technically no benefits, no paid vacations or sick days, no insurance, no Christmas bonuses. Yet, I believe myself to be in the "sweet spot" of God's service and His grace.

I receive phone calls from people each year asking how I do what I do and why. Sometimes they are contemplating stepping out on their own in ministry.

One of my first statements is, "I'll tell you how I do it, then I will share with you what you need to do."

I ask questions that usually cause the caller to pause. "Listen to what I say, not necessarily do what I do" I'll say. "Make sure it is God's calling."

In the end, I share that they must have a precise understanding of what income they must have to live on. Break that down into what you must have per day to live. Then I share with them that they are not going to receive that every day. At best, their earnings days will likely only be about thirty-five to forty percent when their ministry is at full power.

Most working people work, on average, 260 days per year. In the scenario described in the paragraph above, the average days per year of actual paid on the job work is only about 126-140 at best. There may be another forty to sixty days of travel, and the remainder of your time will be preparing, writing, scheduling, and promoting your time and resources. You do not receive pay for these days.

I can paint a bleak financial picture of what this "solo"-type ministry can look like. Several people that I know have tried it over the years and within a year or two they have gone back to serving on church or other denominational entity staff or leaving the ministry for corporate work. There is nothing wrong with working for someone else. Even I work for others. All in ministry work for God. But we all also have others we work for, those who deliver our paycheck.

I had sensed God leading me into this type of ministry setting for several years. I didn't know when and sometimes anticipated it happening in my retirement years. It had never been a clear-cut oration from God. But there were many nuances along the way pointing to this type of ministry setting.

Before stepping out like this, I spoke for a couple of years with others from time to time, men whom I trusted, seeking their input. Again, each time thinking this would likely take place in later years of my life.

One such conversation occurred sitting at breakfast in a hotel restaurant. I shared what I sensed God was moving me toward with my friend, Wayne, whom I had worked with around the nation in conference settings for several years. I had brought Wayne to California to equip some of our leaders. His advice to me, "Don't quit your day job."

Now, Wayne was not saying that I was not good enough or qualified. He was stating that it is an almost impossible task and there are so many uncertainties. He was reminding me of the need for income, insurance, and stability.

Wayne was absolutely right. I gained a lot of valuable insight and encouragement as I spoke with Wayne and others, none of us knowing when God would make the call. My conversations were always, "I believe God is equipping and moving me toward this in the future."

While I know Wayne's assessment was right that morning, when the call came from God, it was definite. There were no doubts. There was no questioning God about finances, benefits or those other things that we often consider essential. Pam and I were both so confident this was God's next calling, there was no need to question anything. God would provide. And He has. We stepped out in faith and followed God in His calling to this ministry. What a blessed ride it has been.

A few years later, I was speaking at a large convention and met up with another friend, Alan, who was speaking at the same convention. I remember us laughing that Saturday morning as he shared, "When you made that move, I was concerned, even worried about you. I was concerned because that is so hard to do. But you proved that God was in it. He has blessed your ministry."

Actually, I have had more than one encounter like the one with Alan. Sometimes they are not as diplomatic as Alan. Some have said things like, "I thought you were crazy when you made that transition," or "I just knew you had lost it (my mind)." Even, "I knew you had to be either one of the biggest men of faith or the craziest men I've ever known."

They used the words "man of faith," but their actual thoughts were likely "I knew you were one of the craziest men I've ever known. Nobody does that!" Indeed, in man's eyes, to leave such a flourishing fruitful ministry for an empty "dream" would seem crazy in our society.

But it was not a dream. It was a calling. God's calling. God's sweet spot of ministry for me in this season of my life. Pam and I were able to make the transition without question because we had seen God at work in our lives throughout our married life. But He never works the same way in these situations. That would remove faith from the equation. We stepped out in faith because God had proven faithful time and time again in our lives.

Pam and I have learned as Paul wrote to the church in Corinth: "By Silvanus, our faithful brother as I consider him, I have written to you briefly, exhorting and testifying that this is the true grace of God in which you stand." (1 Peter 5:12, NKJV).

He has once again proven His grace and faithfulness to us in this absolutely, amazing venture!

Jehovah-Jireh, God's sweet spot is His provision!

Sidenote: Please do not take this as a license to jump into the deep water of a dream or wish — even if it is something you want to do for God.

God desires to bless you through His plans for your life not your wishes or wants.

Frugal Living Doesn't Mean Scraping By

When Pam and I left California to pursue God's next chapter in life, we knew some areas of life would be different. We are both frugal people. We have never lived extravagantly. Quite the opposite actually; we live very conservatively. Yet, starting afresh as an independent contractor in an area where your qualities, skills, and gifts are unknown, is not an easy task. We had been away from Kentucky for more than twenty-two years. When I left in December of 1987, I certainly was not on anyone's radar as a gifted, up-and-coming leader or speaker.

We knew we were doing what God was calling us to, and what He was calling us to was not going to bring instant recognition or financial freedom. In fact, I'm not certain it was ever to bring financial freedom as society defines it.

God's directive was to step out in obedience, following Him with no financial backing. That meant living frugally, cutting back, doing without some things that are not critical for living, even when society tells us otherwise.

I knew it would take three to five years to reach a break-even point. We had only six to eight months of reserve. Once again, it was God calling us to obediently follow Him in faith. Pam and I would talk about this several times before we made the transition from California to Kentucky. Still, it was harder on Pam than she thought it would be. Not in the giving up and living frugally, she was a trooper in those areas — better than me in many ways.

Pam was so frugal, she would go extra hours without eating, waiting to get home rather than stop at fast food and order a sandwich off the dollar menu. Heaven forbid she consider ninety-nine cent fries too. It was harder on her because it took longer to get to that break-even point.

The first five months of 2009, before the transition, our income was a little over $60,000. The remaining seven months, after the move, my earnings totaled $600. Since Pam had not landed a job at this point, that $600 was our total income for the last seven months of 2009.

The first full calendar year of this new ministry venture, God granted me $8,000 in income. The next year, $10,000. For those of you who may be considering branching out on your own — be very sure God is in it and that it is His plan before you make decisions. Ours was less than $20,000 total for two and a half years — well below poverty level. Yet, we did not live in poverty. We never missed a meal, acquired no debt, and never sought any government assistance.

Jehovah-Jireh – God is my provider!

Since that time, there have been some decent years and some not so decent years (in terms of financial remuneration). For more than ten years, I have intentionally paid myself about sixty percent of the national medium personal income rate, just a little over the poverty level. I pay taxes on everything that comes in. But I only pay myself a portion of that amount. Everything else goes back into ministry, helping others.

The couple of times I have reluctantly shared about what I pay myself, the response has been, "There's no way. You cannot possibly live on that."

To which my reply has been, "You may know that, and I may think that, but God does not."

With God all things are possible. Jehovah-Jireh!

I do not share that information to elicit pity or praise. In fact, I have never shared that information anywhere before publicly. I share it here as evidence that we serve a great and faithful God — greater than the financial success of societal thinking.

No money has been placed in my retirement account since leaving California and we continue to live frugally, always looking to cut that which is not required. While living this way is not necessary, it is how we choose to live for Christ.

I have no organization supporting me with benefits or a stipend. Following God's directive into this venture required me saying, "God, I will go to any church, any place, any time you call and lead me as long as I have the resources to get there."

In those twelve plus years, I have never turned any request down. God is our provider and I am extremely grateful for the churches and organizations who provide remuneration for services and resources rendered on behalf of their organization.

Jehovah-Jireh!

Do we have to live this way? No. Could I pay myself more? Yes, I can. But I choose not to. Each year, I am presented with job opportunities to earn more — much more. Several of the opportunities offered have been six-figure income positions.

While those offers are great and demonstrative of the value God has on using my service, thus far, none of those have been God's calling for me. He is still calling me to be obedient in this ministry forum, SonC.A.R.E. Ministries.

Praise God, Pam is a woman who follows God and her husband. Pam has an entry-level clerical position at a hospital. With her job, God provides our insurance benefits and some bill-paying cash.

God's provision is always greater than we can imagine. His provision for us is not about a higher income, it is that He has taught us how to live on much less and serve others.

Jehovah-Jireh!

When we share some of the things we live without, people look at us like a deer staring into headlights, frozen in time. We do not watch much TV, so we only have an antenna, no satellite, no cable, no streaming services, no sports channels. For most purchases, we watch for sales and when we find product that we use, we buy– at sale prices - in larger quantities than most people.

We raise a garden and preserve food, saving us several hundred dollars each year in produce and sauces. We don't eat out much. We've been to maybe six movies in our thirty-two years of marriage. At least half of those were at the invitation of friends, one was a gift and two were with church groups.

While all of this is true, we do not live like sheltered hermits. We enjoy life. Like many people in our culture, we pretty much buy what we want, just not on credit. If we can't pay cash for it within the month, we don't buy it. In these past twelve plus years, we have not missed any payments and looking at my gut, you can tell we do not miss meals. I spend more money than I should on my hobbies each year. We don't live in fear of spending and we do not live off of government subsidies. God is our provider.

Could you live today on less than what you brought home in 1990? We live happily without debt, all on an income that would cause some to say "Impossible!"

I challenge that word with this emphatic statement: "Nothing is impossible with God" (Luke 1:37). Our obedience to God allows us the privilege to live an incredibly happy, fruitful life. And we live it realizing the love of money and materialism is not the answer, though we have been immensely blessed materially.

Obedience to God is the answer. If God says you can live without it, trust Him — you can live without it! We enjoy God-provided freedoms that most people cannot fathom.

Jehovah-Jireh!

Love of the Outdoors From my Dad and My Heavenly Father

I love the outdoors! That is probably an understatement. From my earliest memories, I've always enjoyed being outside. As a child in the summer, I'd get up, fly down the stairs, quickly eat a bowl of cold cereal and out the door I went.

I'd be out there until lunch, back out until supper, and after chores in the kitchen, back out until dark. On really fortunate days, Mom would bring sandwiches outside for lunch on the picnic table.

As I grew, I gained an even deeper love for the outdoors. Primarily thanks to my mom and dad. My parents loved to fish and camp. Every Spring Break, rain or shine, we went camping at one of the state park lakes in Kentucky. Every weekend Dad could manage to get away, we went camping and fishing. Every vacation was a guaranteed week at the lake.

Honestly, I was a teenager before I realized the words vacation and camping were not synonymous. I thought they were the same. I did not know you could go anywhere else on vacation.

My brothers and I were not allowed to play little league baseball because it would interfere with weekend fishing trips. I would have loved to play baseball, but I enjoyed camping and fishing so much that I never missed baseball. We did play in church leagues some years and the church coaches knew that camping came first.

I have many great memories of those trips to the lake. All seven of us camping in a tent or sleeping with my brother Bill in a Conestoga-type wagon (a tarp covered trailer) while the rest of the family slept in the tent.

Memories of fishing throughout the day and into the night. Memories of Dad still sitting at the campfire after everyone else went to bed. Dad being the first one up at the fire every morning before daylight. Memories of all our meals being cooked over an open fire. Perhaps that is why I still love to cook outside and do so quite often. If you could experience the feeling that I have just recalling some of those memories.

As us boys got a little older, Dad would share with us another of his outdoor loves: hunting. He began by taking one or more of us with him squirrel or rabbit hunting.

We were only spectators, on those first trips. There he would teach us some of the basics of hunting squirrels or rabbits. Later, Dad would take us out to a friend's farm and teach us to shoot. We were never allowed to touch a firearm until he had instilled in us proper firearm handling and safety. He was very stern and meticulous in this — as he should have been.

From that point on, at least for my oldest brother and me, we were hooked. Today, I still love fishing and being outside. But nothing surpasses my love for hunting.

I mainly hunt deer these days. Venison (deer meat) is leaner and healthier than beef, and I love to share venison with others. There is always family and friends waiting for the spoils of the hunt. I only shoot what I or others will eat. Well, I'll admit that I might shoot a coyote or raccoon on occasion.

But greater than my love for fishing, hunting, and the outdoors was the love my dad instilled in me for the Creator of the outdoors.

The reason I love hunting so much, deer hunting especially, is that it is a time and place to be still and alone with God in His beautiful sanctuary. While hunting season is mainly in the fall and early winter months, I will go walk in the woods, perhaps climb into a tree stand, throughout the year, just to spend time with God in that most relaxing atmosphere — His sanctuary. In the off season, you might even catch me singing to our God while sitting in a tree.

Whether the trees in the woods are budding in the spring, lush with green leaves and shade in the summer, filled with beautiful colors of autumn or barren in the midst of winter, they are always a beautiful, comforting sight to me.

Driving down the road in the winter past a wooded area of barren trees against an overcast gray sky with a bedding of brown dead leaves would seem to most people dreary and blight. But to me it is an exhilarating, breathtaking scene. A beauty of God's design. A venue calling out to me.

I was hunting on my brother-in-law's farm a few years ago. When I came in after dark, he was outside with a flashlight behind one of his barns waiting, watching for me. He asked, "Have you been out there all day?"

My car was sitting in front of his barn, so he assumed I had been. "Since an hour before daylight," I reported.

To which he replied, "I could not do it. I don't see how you can do it."

My response was, "Pam will tell you that I cannot sit still for fifteen minutes the rest of the year. But when I get out there with God, I can sit all day." And indeed, I do. I carry a camera or two with me now and shoot video of deer more than I actually shoot for the meat.

God's word, The Holy Bible shares His six days of creation. God gave mankind dominion over all the earth, the beasts of the field, the birds of the air, the fish of the sea, and the crops in the field. God's creation is for our provision and includes areas such as the Garden of Eden, the first place He gave Adam and Eve to live and enjoy while building their relationship with God above.

Yes, God can meet you in the church. He can meet you in your prayer closet, in your car, home, or anywhere you will join Him. I spend time with Him in all of those places. Though my favorite place is in the midst of His creation, in the woods, perhaps sitting in a tree communing with Him, both talking to Him and listening to His response. Simply taking in the beauty of His creation and the aroma of his presence.

I am grateful to my mother and father for teaching me to love the Creator and His creation. I am especially grateful for them teaching me the love of the outdoors and I relish every minute I get to spend with our Heavenly Father outside.

God has graciously provided all of His great and beautiful creation for us to enjoy with Him.

Jehovah-Jireh.

Closing

There are many more life lessons from God that I could write about. Important lessons for me from God and those whom He used to teach me.

Some of those people are heroes, others God used to teach me vulnerability and to remind me of my shortcomings.

Some of you have received a copy of this book because God has used you to influence and teach me. I am grateful for each person God has used to help me along my life journey. I'm certain God has used some, perhaps many, people in my life who I had no clue He was using. For every person God used I am grateful, and I pray they get to read this even if they are already in heaven.

This book was written not as a way to brag about myself. I know who I am in Christ and I know who I would be without Christ in my life. This book was written to encourage its readers in hopes that every reader will live a godly life, encouraging others as you seek God's lessons in your own life.

He is a great God, and He has made a way for you and I to enjoy His presence on this earth and for all eternity in heaven through the shed blood and sacrifice of His one and only Son Jesus Christ.

He made the sacrifice, but the choice to accept or refuse His plan of redemption is up to each one of us to make. I cannot make the decision for you. You cannot make the decision for your brother, your spouse, your children, or anyone else. Each person must make the decision in his or her own life.

We have a decision to make because we have all sinned. Sin is any act that displeases God. Just as a child will act in ways that displeases his or her parents, so some of our actions displease God. Our sin nature has separated us from God and only God could make a way of redemption, reclaiming our relationship with Him. This is what He did through Jesus Christ.

To accept His plan of redemption is a decision of the heart, not the mind. We each must first recognize that we are sinners. There must be a burning desire to turn away from all sinful ways — all things displeasing to God — and invite His Holy Spirit into the heart to assist in living a godly life.

Godly life is not about rituals such as a walk down an aisle in a church service or getting baptized. It is not about church attendance or money given or being good. Those are not my words, but God's. Read His word, The Holy Bible, and see for yourself. Someone has said, "Good people don't get into heaven. Redeemed people get into heaven."

Jehovah-Jireh, God, has provided the only plan of redemption for all mankind. The decision to accept or reject God's plan lies on each one of us. What is your decision?

May God use this book to influence you in encouraging others as you live your life for Him!

I cannot say it enough: He is a great God providing for us in so many ways as we walk life's road. His lessons are great, timely, and timeless. Seek out His wonderful life lessons on your journey. He has provided them for you.

After all, He is Jehovah-Jireh.

More resources from George Yates and SonC.A.R.E. Ministries

Turnaround Journey: Discovering a Path for Effective leadership Embedded in this story are important principles about actually leading an organization to plan and implement strategic change. Many churches & organizations plan, but there is large difference between planning and strategic planning for implementation and effective results. Learn more at: http://soncare.net/turnaround-journey/

Reaching the Summit: Avoiding and Reversing Decline in the Church – Straight forward, practical, this book is a down to earth analysis of why so many churches are in decline and what to do about it. Methodically works through the five phases of decline the book then turns to the process of identifying the principles and strategies for "Reversing and Avoiding Decline." Learn more at: http://soncare.net/reaching-the-summit/

Teaching That Bears Fruit is teaching that produces true learning – life changing learning. This work looks at the methods Jesus used to create lasting learning in His listeners. Powerful enough to turn the world upside down. Jesus' teachings are still transforming lives more than 2,000 years later. An indispensable book for anyone who loves to teach the Bible. Learn more at: http://soncare.net/teaching-that-bears-fruit/

Coaching is one of the greatest tools we have in leading others. We are all leaders in some area of our lives. This book is written in particular for those in leadership in business and ministry. Yet every person can gain great insights from this book. Coaching is a very effective type of leadership. The greater your coaching abilities become the more effective leader you will become.

Revealed inside are the hidden values of two very important factors of life and leadership. https://soncare.net/coaching-a-way-of-leadership-a-way-of-life

Whether you are leading a church, business, or fortune 500 company, successful leaders are continuously working, studying to improve their leadership skills. Improving your leader skills helps you become a better leader and equips you to build other leaders. Investing a minimum of seven minutes each day can improve your leadership and the effectiveness of your organization.

Made in the USA
Monee, IL
26 August 2021